Literary Magazine

GROSSMONT COLLEGE

GROSSMONT-CUYAMACA
COMMUNITY COLLEGE DISTRICT

The Acorn Review is a student-led course in reviewing, editing, and publishing works contributed by the greater San Diego community. While *Acorn Review* accepts submissions from all ages and residents of San Diego County, most submissions come from students of the Grossmont College Creative Writing, English, and Visual Arts programs.

Faculty and Administrators

The Acorn Review editorial staff wishes to thank the following people who helped make this issue possible:

Professors Karl Sherlock, Daniela Sow, Ryan Griffith, Juliana Cárdenas, Adam Deutsch, Enrique Cervantes, Richard Farrell, and Alan Traylor.

Editorial Staff

Liz Aguilar
Abdullah Al Ghanimi
Amber Baker
Jamilah Barajas
Tasha Bonsignore
Renee Brower
Olivia Bylsma
Shahin Elihu
Beth Ferris
Emme Fugate
Angelica Garcia Diaz
Disney Green
Joseph Houser
Paul Katz
Alexis Lopez
Michele Magnuson
Cameron McGowan
Damia Meglasson
Matteo Mendoza
Dee Richards
Hannah Ross
Jose Trujillo
Jasmine Valdez

Design & Layout by Michele Magnuson

Note from the Editor

My tenure as a student in the *Acorn Review* course ended in the Fall of 2019, but I wasn't quite ready to let go. So, I stuck around for the Spring and volunteered, once again, to take on designing the layout for this issue of the magazine. It truly is a labor of love and I am so grateful to have my name attached to this collection in multiple forms. By the time I finish reading, editing, and organizing everything, I feel as though I've been given a little peak into everyone's creative soul, and I believe that makes me the most fortunate member of the editorial staff. But as I wrap up my time with *Acorn*, I look forward to finishing a Master of Fine Arts program with Queens University of Charlotte with the intention of once again returning to Grossmont, but this time in the role of an educator. So, as I bid you all a fond, and temporary, farewell, I would like to say thank you. To the faculty and administration, to my fellow editors, to our contributors, and to our readers: Thank You.

Sincerely,
Michele Magnuson

COVER

Mario Loprete *b-boy; oil on concrete*

CONTENTS

Poetry

ART

FEATURED ARTIST

PROSE

EXTRAS

POETRY

Dorothe Bonsignore

-submitted posthumously by her daughter, Tasha Bonsignore

Sonnet

Where bougainvillea weep magenta blooms
upon the shadowed tiles of Spanish clay—
open doors to empty courtyard rooms
view filigree that's crumbled to decay;
and shafts of sun no longer pierce the panes
of Tyrian purple glass now hid by leaves.
Along this haunted walk my heart restrains
from shouting, --as a frightened Queen deceives
her enemies with chary, prudent smile.
Once, within this shadowed, cloistered place,
I loved him, and the garden was in style—
and greedily we clung in close embrace.

But now my path, with bougainvillea's flood,
staining all the patterned tiles like blood.

Upon the Death of a Fisherman

With brown and naked backs they dug his place
upon the barren cliff above the sea.
The widow bathed and laid him out, her face
like polished clay. Her hands dropped awkwardly
into her lap, strangers on their backs,
while tapers burned all night around his head,
filling unmatched saucers up with wax;
dawn comes late, when waiting with the dead.

They bore him open, up the tangled trail
and set his heavy coffin on the mound.
Seagulls, startled by the driven nail,
pierced the sky, and shovels sealed the ground;
while down upon the cove with half-crossed oar,
"Socorro" drifted, empty, by the shore.

Upon the Death of Ernest Hemingway

The boulders burst and lift the swelling waves
and heave their giant backs against the spray,
like naked eunuchs bowed, these stony slaves,
enduring silently as they betray
their apathy in soul-less, chafing death.
With swollen breast the pounding tide assuages
where it wounds, with soothing spindrift breath,
measuring out the dying time in ages.

Like massive crags our lives erode away,
so slowly scarred that we have brief regret,
until like eagles we ascend the sea
and what we were is sand upon the shore
that whirls with tempests, willingly and free.
We die each hour until at last we soar!

Egor Reading at Bahia de Los Angeles

Tasha Bonsignore

Tasha Bonsignore

Memorial Day

Within the terror of bullets throbbing into the earth around them,
a mate's body thrust, tossed, topples – torn apart.
They say there are no atheists in foxholes.
Superstitious soldier swears by protective amulet, bracelet,
picture, bible,
talisman fending off the festering fear. The damn deep six
drama.

Kill the other human before they kill you, dead to the notion of
people
on the other side of the explosive device defiantly detonated.
Sad euphemisms erupt with war, sanitizing the hellish
consequences.

Posthumous Medal of Valor, Service Cross, Silver Star,
the war widow stares at a coin of metal, a snippet of ribbon
floating in her tear stained hands.

Amulets, talismans, thoughts and prayers.
Thank you for your service,
sorry for your loss.

Haleiwa Hawaii

Tasha Bonsignore

Shahin Elihu

Alive

My heart is like a bird with broken wings
colorful feathers red, blue, yellow, green,
no damn good

like a ship at edge of sea
with storm of Noah,
needs ark to survive the hurricane

like a sitar with torn strings
Ravi Shankar crying

sound of no music
no eyes to see
to hear no ears
no feet to walk
to wash no hands

lung to breathe
a mind to think
hope to live

Humanity

In reality we were humans
then race cut our connection
religion, separated from each other
politics, erected wall between us
wealth made classes out of us
all wanted freedom
without knowing what is slavery
captivity is not bars around us
fortification around our thinking

Respect

HAIKU: From Ferdowsi Author of the Shahnameh (Book of King)

Don’t hurt an ant
it hauls a grain for its soul
the happy life is sweet

Black cruel spirited man
which wanted harm an alive ant
sick enjoys the deed

The Nature

Pain like dust arrived from all directions
sat on the head, eye and while on face
when deeds ended
came back with respect
rested on both knees

Island of the Dancers

Tasha Bonsignore

Beth Ferris

Corona-Cast Shadows

Here we are
shackled to our homes
lost in isolation,
edgy with free-fall thoughts,
unused to idle hands and
subdued tongues.
The squirrel cage rattles on.

The garden once
a burdensome chore,
now a sigh of release
from stale confines.
Lush lavender blossoms
nod in tranquil grace,
fig trees unfurl massive fronds
contending for her golden rays
like gladiators in the colosseum.
While we of pallid faces
seek remedy from
our domestic catacombs.

We struggle to remember
how to be alone
with ourselves,
without each other.
Forgotten is the resonance
of our inner voice,
minds like fallow fields
rotting with disuse.
Alone with mirror-rendered façade,
a stranger glares back at us.

Time, once valued,
now stretched thin,
like spindled-thread,
on the verge of fraying.

These unfettered moments
resounding in our minds
like the clatter of pebbles
within an empty pale.
Our empty hands
grasp for phantom palms,
our blue-dimmed sight
beholden to glass-glared screens
seeking reconnection

In stillness, we stand together
while the world holds its breath
waiting to begin anew
on the other side of this shadow

Lilliana's Sestina

Lillianna was born china-doll perfect;
flamed-red curls, rose-petal lips, eyes of jade green.
Her pristine-white complexion made porcelain weep.
For her long-fingered hands, the piano begged, "please tickle our keys."
But she stood alone, her plain-faced family, unable to embrace
her exquisite nature; their affections stunted by what they envied.

One day in the forest, Lillianna drawn to all she was denied, a harmony she envied.
Leaves rejoicing in their variety, pirouette for the wind; a dance so perfect.
The sun-peppered depths, warmed radiance, inviting her embrace.
A festival of verdant growth, an extended family of multi faceted green,
roots sunk deep, intertwined in kindred explorations, like keys
locked into the rich soil; an accord so precious it made her weep.

An obsidian-eyed dove, snow-feathered, settles near her, "Why do you weep?"
Startled into a reply, "This forest's tolerance to all diversity; a family envied,
one I wish to share. To shed human form, becoming sister, holds the keys
to a life without loneliness. To become part of something greater, this perfect.
place, to thrive, nourished by the sun's warmth, nurtured in all this green,
roots and branches for extremities, leaves impeccably poised in perpetual embrace."

The dove, feeling the girl's pain, covers her scarlet head with one of its wings, an embrace
meant to comfort, merely a ploy to hide her own urge to weep.
"Never have I met a human with such need to be bound to the living green.
I respect your convictions, though strangely precocious, are not

to be envied.
I would help you if I could. But there is only one answer to this perfect
conundrum; a special kind of magic to provide you with those keys".

"Wait for the full moon of Samhain, seek the emerald fairy who holds these magic keys.
I must warn you, the forest demands a sacrifice: to take you into their embrace,
you must relinquish your humanity, for your joining to be without fault, to be perfect.
No longer will you walk the land or speak. Your eyes will not see as they once did, nor weep."
The dove, saddened, shakes her head, sympathizing, a plight too bleak to be envied,
Lillianna lifts her head high, eyes bright, glowing in a hopeful shade of green.

On the night of Samhain's bloated moon, the forest becomes a silent altar of green.
The emerald fairy forewarned of the girl's request, holds in her pale hands the keys
to Lillianna's transformation. The whole of the forest awaits the ritual with envied
breath, to witness her transcendence, a form none can guess. She endures the magical embrace.
With petals white and raven-red, leaves of jaded-green.
Welcoming their new sister, happily they weep.
Once girl, now graceful orchid, swaying with primal elegance, content, her life now perfect.

For the family who envied, blinded to love, trapped in a jealous miasma of vicious green,
could not accept Lillianna for her perfect grace. In their ignorance, realized too late the keys
to nurturing, unable to yield to her embrace; now bow their heads, in her absence they weep.

Poe: Perversely Cursed

Gothic's father, horror's mother.
Mapping a conduit to the dark side of psyche pain,
exposing nightmares beyond Grimm's tales.
Freud's translations unbound

Idle thoughts of immortality conflict
with random acts of murder.
Pounding mortal hearts, a cliché of phobia's
in Poe's new providence...

We chase our fears into the darkness,
where we hide from the faintness of our souls.
A frenzied ecstaticity of catharsis or
a calculated mathematical composition.

He made our hands shake,
raised the hairs on the backs of our necks.
His prose, devotees to aberrancy;
only the most deviant graced his path.

Poe's art emulates life.
Deviation, addiction, and death;
where the imp reigns supreme.
Perversity decrees adversity;
he dies alone and in pain

The Year of Bodily Conflict

Proverbs are to pain
    as pills to forgetting:
a dim hope that tomorrow
    will not be the same.

Still the pain invades,
    my thoughts and dreams
like cockroaches in the kitchen;
little malignant-brown fuckers
    popping up with a persistence
    that is almost, admirable.

Lightning cascades up my spine
    in jagged strikes,
disproving the laws of physics;
its repetition cruelly strategic
    seeking a surrender
    I refuse to give.

I will not accept an invalid's status:
    impotent, useless.
For now, my will remains my own;
    to do battle, or withdraw,
    tomorrow is a gift
    not to be squandered.

Without Susan

Broken-winged wren
flew a path to hermitage
preferring obscurity over notoriety,
alone in a world too-soon-born-to; her art
misunderstood, misread, unacknowledged.

Her byzantine thoughts bent in concentric notions,
interconnected, like wild crop circles,
colored by somber images; death
leaving its indelible mark in the
darkened mirror of her reflection.

Searching for passion,
realizing only one-sided devotions,
her hollowed-heart, a list of omitted names.
What became of Susan? Now an erasure in
the journals of her empty life.

Her mind, verging on the Spectrum;
few fathomed how she saw the world.
Connecting the obtuse with paisleyed-prose,
defying classical conventions.
She taught us all,
how to think outside
the box

Ruinas en San Blas

Tasha Bonsignore

Chelsey Gable

A Spectrum Oppressor

Nine years of no sound
like a blank sheet of paper
untainted by those that roam
London's streets, New York skyline
a decade delineated in minutes
Swirling wings entrust flight to pen
Across eighteen feet of canvas
windows and columns nothing is missing-
except the melody of I Am Happy

Death of a Cherished King

An erasure poem: Text taken from *The Wife of Bath's Prologue* by Jeffrey Chaucer.

Of wives, While corpses lay
Husbands slept and some
in this world of grass or herbs
better than a brawling, wicked, contrarious husband:

~~With his fist he struck me on the head,~~
"~~He came to me and near me he knelt down,~~
~~What I have done, you are to blame therefor.~~

When I saw he'd never make it
I snatched and tore.
such a blow
And on the floor I lay dead
kiss me before I die He said; so
help me God now I will die
with much woe

We made it up
Between ourselves and so
he put my book gathered unto me-
as the term of all life;
after that day
never any so was he to me

I pray in majesty.
Bless his soul now
Will you hear

Flailing Arms

Puckered lines pulling and pink from edge to end
Crusty and purple--blood is clotting
Vitreous with patches of fresh tearing
have I ever cared if people stare
at my face tiny nails raked across
Wrathful at the disfigurement
Even more so that infancy is brief

Honestly

Spumescent blue boils over the pyramids, maybe
I'll write her a note that's kind
of about pandas who are refusing bamboo
"It's not being digested well" they say
we can't stomach it. There's no nutrients
for someone so full of fluff 'n stuff
that I don't want to hear, but
you're either a carnivore or an herbivore
So, I guess just stick with being bitchy

The Meat Counter

The Butcher was born
some will have a slice of cake-
while Picts plot on empty bellies

Cattle and men
will be slaughtered
equally under his knife

Their carcass should be wrapped
in variegated cloth
instead of brown paper

A rib, a leg,
a side of meat
for sale by the pound

Hoards of flesh sent abroad
for profiteering
by America's Union Jack

Maybe Tudors should
disclose to their pupils
Dead subjects always comply

Aguascalientes French Quarter Angels

Fabian Diaz Luevano

Angelica Garcia Diaz

How I Love Her

I lover her the way popcorn kernels love to get
stuck between molars. The way socks like
to get lost during laundry until there's not a
single matching pair in sight. The way alarm
clocks love to not go off when you most need
them to.

I love her.

I love her when it's ten minutes past the time we
were supposed to leave the apartment and she's
standing five-foot-four in mismatched socks, trying
to dig kernels out from between her teeth because
microwaved popcorn was all we had time to cook
in the morning.

I love her.

OB Sun

Tay Heylman

F.C. George

at the center

But there she knits her cloudy universe.
Exactly where, a simple guess;
no world beyond its reach. Her
game from unexplained horizons
outside the silky spin. Inviting soft
her satellite of sticky fuzz. Soon
in the dish, a creature lands,
barbaric, yet Cyclosa, without thought,
inhales it, to make what was her own.

Her hammock holds a decoy spider,
fungus covered shells of prior prey,
recycled in the emptiness of yearly round.
Shaking in webbed dangle the tiny architect
trampolines the bigger one to life. In
stretchy bounce the inner space raws open, full
exposed it aches for fill with any truth, a
bind to others drifting by. Perchance
with luck, all colors blend to clear and
broken light in mirrored fascination-awing smiles
as liquid as the mirage of lights itself that
hang in tears against the woven shredded sky.

(unborn)

The Heparin flush, cold and salty speeding,
burning through my veins, ending
on tongue's tip. IV-shivers pushed up right behind.

Orangey the next flood - 2-liter bags
of vitamin infused Saline - to water
the flowering baby, rain on his "calm" world,
there, in the dark of monotone shushes,
of dark fleshy warmth, and infrequent hiccups.

On the outside, tremors answer
the sudden life-sustaining wave: shakes
of sugar-high that no insulin can cope.
Where dry heaves exhausted now

watery calm. Washed away the nights
of near collapse, close to own
starvation, the bulging body. Organs
now quenched and prepped to sustain
the life, to do their deed.

your time

Outside, a final pile-up of cars
cramped into the tiny driveway,
when the last train gets delayed. With
no expectancy of time or destination.
Sure, it will come,
rather soon and
you will get on it, with
your pre-paid ticket and
personalized seat assignment. Maybe
even First Class with a welcome cocktail.
For now, - it's late! and
you wait, awake to another
day with the same far
hectic traffic noise, the
staleness in the air, and the
dried up words on your lips, staring
at the same mountains in the distance.

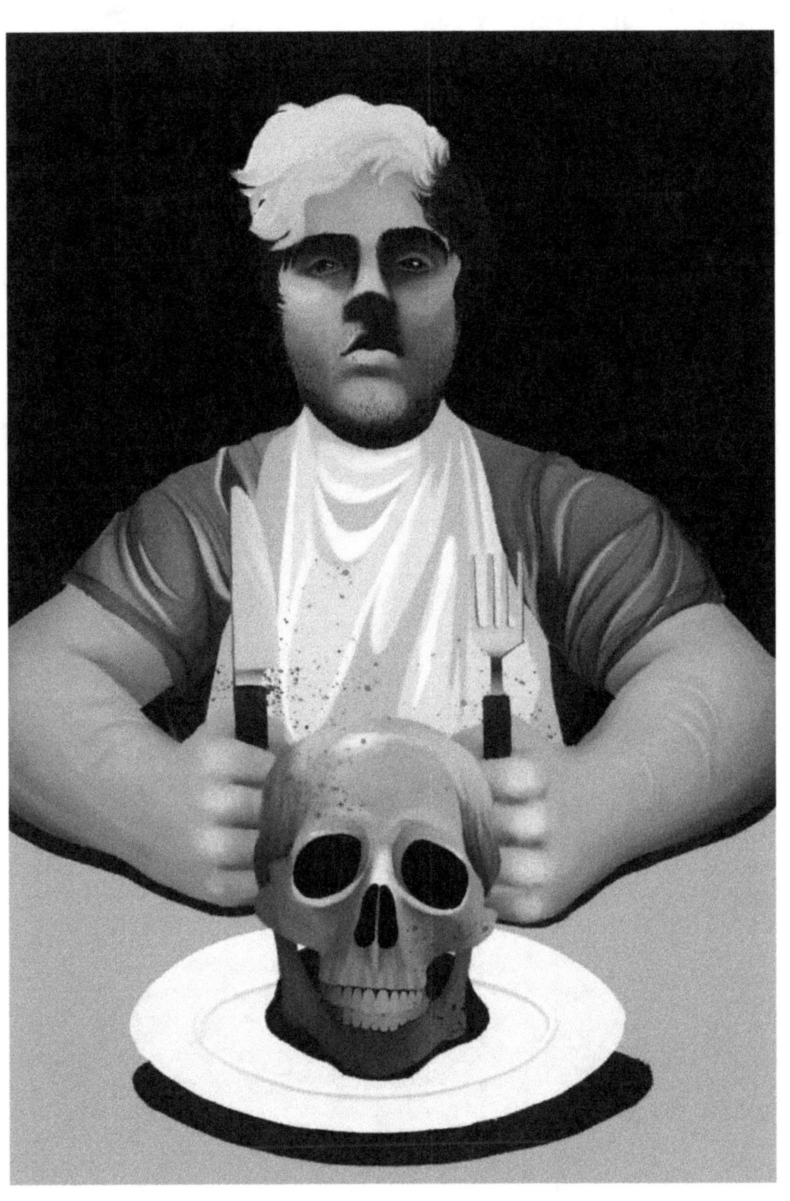

Hunger
Cameron McGowan

Reina Hearts

Adults

do not be deceived
just "mature" children raising
immature people

On "So Many Feelings" by EARTHGANG

I feel like an underage sonnet
forced to date a drunken haiku
in this free form state.

I feel like improvised lyrics
that can never procreate
with my ex-spouse Paper.

I feel like the new mainstream underground sleeper
without the recognition.

I feel like a monologue
at CliffsNotes speed.

I feel like the number 96
on opposite ends of our bed.

I feel like I'm too girly to be a woman
but too manly to be seen as one.

I feel a song that storms brains with pre-dawn popcorn
As it loops around any water
Falling out of pase.

Bee Steps
Tim Mountain

Merrienne Jimenez

The Parts I Remember

Eyes—quaint as almonds,
paired with primmed brows,
peeking through the rearview
mirror, glass reflecting glass,
squinting through haze, struggling to
remain in the present
with me.

Arm—bent at the elbow, perched
over the edge of the driver's window,
welcoming gusts of wind that swaddle my
ears with sweet somethings, rake
through my wisps of hair, weaving
with silvery clouds, a feeling I
could never earn
from her.

Hands—cool as ceramic, tawny
tones too powerful to hide
behind cloth, stifling my
surroundings, a smoldering blanket
of warmth that she wrapped
around everyone
but me.

Fingertips—dipped in deep red,
sculpted specially for a cigarette
to rest seamlessly between her
middle and pointer fingers, a
cradle of comfort, sparking
a joy I could never provide
for her.

Grass and Wind

Tim Mountain

Michele Magnuson

64.599442, -21.836528

I have seen the beginning
where my history was present.
Where Vóden predated Odin.
Where the euhemerism
leads back to Priam in Greece.

Now a church, an unmarked
road off Þjóðvegur
and west of Hvítur,
where Snorri found his Edda.

Snuffed out by Christianity,
alluded to in days -
Thursday Thor's day,
Wednesday Odin's day.

Bibliomaniac

Living in worlds constructed
through liquid dried on pulp.
Fabricating her fortress
with lexicons and tomes
taken from discarded libraries.

Captivated by tales
replete with accounts
of lives more restrained;
corrupted by fiction,
Waiting for Darcy.

The decomposing pages
her only liberation
from the commotion
of her own story.

Coccyx

The scars he will leave
are deeper than skin.
Outer marks, nothing
compared to the marks
etched within, like notches
in a bedpost when he
breaks you. As you
breathe and push, he
will crack your coccyx.
And when they pull you
from the earth everyone
will know what you did.

e.e. – a ghazal

Stand next to me when I look at you –
the hair in my skin reaching to you.

Flush my veins to heat my breath
as I lose inhibition in the dream of you.

Gasp your name through fingertips
while I pretend to taste you.

Wet the cotton beneath me
without touching you.

Waiting for *he* to ask "may I touch it" –
waiting for *he* to be you.

Harfluenzis

There is a landscape
that swallows my now,
takes back thirteen years
depleted by motherhood.

The honeyed sweat
pools in her forest,
the dense black curl
of her velvet crown.

Tresses unfurling
to perfume my world,
sleek black smoke
ameliorates discontent.

Intense Dark 60% Cacao

Once rich in essence,
melting on contact
with finger or tongue.
Now half white, dried.
Flavorless beige dust.
Leaving me
disappointed, wishing
I had opened it sooner,
when I was younger;
had the whole of time
to study it,
savor it,
devour it.

The Passion Flower of the Sherlock

Tim Mountain

Ricardo Martinez

To Susan

Mes livres sont sois la table:
French and Shakespeare.
I put them there with my poetry
and doubt that I will
take them out tonight.
It's Friday…
in one hour
I'll be at the airport
to say goodbye to you
but I'd rather not go…

When I look at your painted portrait,
I remember carefully placing
each stroke upon the canvas.
But as I look at it now,
I know I've failed:
the eyes are as bland
as the brown moles on my arm,
the cheeks blush around your smile
like the rouge on a mime,
and the hair is coarse
like the "devil's hair"
that grows on canyon brush.

As I look at the candle
fluttering on the table,
I imagine us at the airport:
I hear us talking about
skiing in the mountains,
watching the swallows
return to San Juan Capistrano,
or the horned toads scatter
as we hike on a summer path,
and viewing the colored leaves
falling from the trees in Vermont.
I also imagine us sitting there

not knowing what to say,
waiting for the intercom to announce:
"Flight 547 is ready for departure."
And I blow out the candle
as I watch you go.

Vigil

Another senseless slaughter
followed by a vigil to honor
the memories of the victims.
The light from the flames of the candles
reflects against the solemn faces
of the crowd and disappears
into the night. Their prayers
momentarily break the silence
but when they finish and disperse
the silence and darkness return.

Annoyed

Hannah Ross

Cameron McGowan

Abuser

I held your hand
as you took your first steps,
helping you find a path
that you felt was safe enough
until you knew it well enough
to step forward on your own.

You kissed my cheek
at the event you'd invited yourself to,
leaving behind the shape of you
in bloody red lipstick,
a mark that I can't scrub away
even though I've tried.

Your left-behind belongings
were a scourge on me,
one that screeched the memories
we made together
until they felt like
venom in my veins.

The promises you broke
still echo sometimes,
reverberating in my skull
that you can't be trusted,
and I never should have
given you that power.

"Are we not friends anymore?"

For the first time,
you'd given me something
and when the shackles
finally came loose,
I could feel freedom again.

Brother with Guitar
Hannah Ross

Jay Mower

Ancient Sailor's Cry

A tsunami of torment flows through
these old patched sails while the sun
of yesterday sets beyond the cove.

She cruises my sea of gone in *Prada* fashions,
steered by an *Armani* arm as I mend canvas
that will see only a few more moons.

On knee bent, I cry on a reef of hope
when she kindly replies, *I admire, trust*
and am fond of you, yet can pretend no more.

She sails, leaving a whirlpool of woe.
India ink records what only water
remembers at the next whitecap.

James Patrick Rodey Editors' Choice Award – Poetry

Bending Reality

I love the word nelipot, and it has a solid etymology
from the Greek for "barefoot"...
--Other-Wordly website

Tired of goofy words, my iPad nods off. I pass
kaleidoscope oils that pop off white studio walls
and nelipot down a spiral staircase where
brown, yellow, red, black and white men,
dressed in stark penguin attire, chauffeur
multi-hued taffeta and chiffon across parquet
under crystal chandeliers to a big band beat
conducted by Glen Miller's phantasmal baton.

I muster enough *chutzpah* to tango
with a *Dior-draped* dish languishing
on the sidelines. She ignores my odd attire
and performs majestically, scenting
my senses with *Chanel,* as we summon
stares from dancers and musicians alike.
Yet, the beat continues until I feel a tap
on my left shoulder and a lavish

Veronica Lake-blonde cuts in, airs
her *Lancôme* fragrance and completes
our folk ballet with a horizontal dip.
Chest to breast, cheek-to-cheek, we linger
and I yearn for more as the chandelier dims
and we drift into a land of rainbows.
The vanilla with patchouli deep notes,
orange taste of fuchsia lips, supple fabric

of her skin and warmth of her heartbeat
pounding my torso, vanquish all inhibitions.
Her tresses flow as she melts below
in my arms and reality's bent beyond
human recognition, then I sense feelings
temporal as that waft of *Lancôme* vanishes.

She fades supine into the parquet while
I float above to the rainbow chandelier.

Coming Home

Homage to Robert Frost

He enjoys chill darkness, no shadows as strands
of black capellini sparkle rime on tarmac.

His life roils like a sackful of mallets, his quest,
a backpack full of snakes and pockets of potential.

The dead lurk in his dreams, become white tigers
harrying him to dawn before he turns and chases them.

With memories churning in empty rooms,
he looks backward with pride, forward with hope.

In clandestine lands with flowers thick like mist,
he perceives a thousand people with one face.

Troubled when two opposite things are true,
he's consoled by warm thoughts of home.

When you return to the hearth in frost, they must
take you in, even with a shadow over your breath.

Dante's Advice For Young Princes

Obvious as a lion
tending herds of gnus,
some tongues wag slander,
the bold resort to assassination
and the devious ostracize.

Instead, I mix oak galls, wine
and vinegar, quill
venom over velum
while my ink horn
pumice stone and knife
rest at my side, eternally
impugn names of men who
harm, sully or disparage me,

use media to show Charon
pole a punt of select souls
across the Styx. Burn corrupt clerics
in sand and rain, repay wrathful
Filippo's slap and lies as he gurgles
under foul water and flame heretic
Farinata in his fiery tomb.
Though still alive, I prepare
a filthy ditch for the simoniac
Pope Boniface VIII to circle
forever in leaden robes.

Modern times call for clever ways
to wrest power, but if you rule lands
of heathens, contact fellow Fiorentini,
Niccolò Machiavelli. Though younger
than I am, he has many excellent ideas
on how to prosper.   Ciao.

Migraine

Skin sagging, an older woman and man, both nude,
mud-wrestle in swine squalor at the intersection
of Government Avenue and Money Boulevard.

A shrieking media pundit blathers
at another blathering colleague,
discord pounds my pores at 110 decibels.

Reality Television, Facebook and Twitter
trump Internet fundraising and the mass media,
just like Kennedy on TV overpowered radio.

Pressure thunders through my unsettled brain
like click-clacking freight trains running amok.
Pain pounds from temple to ear drum.

My gut roils insecure when know-nothings
advocate extreme positions, appear to rule
the mood in much of Middle America

Uncertainty, reckless policies and glamour
over-shadowing substance, churn my bowels,
as a victor emerges from the mire.

A mad dog barks. Wavy lines, flashing lights
and pain engulf the back of my eyes. I see 3-D
zigzags, an intense aura with white and dark dots.

Storms swallow left eye and a dragon
flashes in front of my good right eye
while I race for the Excedrin.

Wistful Love

Yesterday is dead and gone
And tomorrow's out of sight...
Kris Kristofferson lyrics

Rain sheets my windowpane.
A distance wordless call whispers,
cries *never too late*, yet here I wait
for a sign to prod me to what I deny.

Though I was born too soon for any
encounter to bloom, she captivates
my mind when we meet over dogs,
furry ones, at the neighborhood park.

Perky shape, blondish hair
and an enchanting beam halos her,
sure, she's made several spins
around the sun, but gentle ones.

Though I cannot tell how words began,
yet magnetic waves pulsed through me.
We talk of dogs, children and mention
significant others to show *no hit intended.*

When she did suggest we meet,
walk the canyon together,
I brighten, even though I know
the relationship cannot grow.

As the rain sheets this window, my pain
realizes how important to enjoy
the present moment, hope for more
and not telescope a future that cannot be.

Gaby
Hannah Ross

E.R. O’Connor

Madame Mercury’s Traveling Creepshow: Apophenia

come one,
come all.

prepare to witness
sweet Apophenia,
perplexed,
in a state
of perpetual
paranoia, feigning
and frightening
her demons.

she neither
sobs
nor screams, yet,
pareidolia
stakes its
putrid claim —
cackling cacophonies
over rigored cadavers.

watch her
foam at the mouth,
as she slices open
strained skin,
and offers flesh
to slimy spiders
from a pool
of black blood.

blink, and
she’s gone.

Madame Mercury's Traveling Creepshow: Siamese Twins

come one,
come all.

beckon your children
behind you,
they make
bounteous
delectable snacks
for our
siamese twins,
Sage and Sarabella.

pry open your pupils
and ogle
as they are
swallowed whole,
bones bent backwards,
brandishly beheaded —
slipping from cupid's bow
to adam's apple.

creep a peak
at their blind
blank eyes,
benevolent and beastly
behind blooding bandages,
at their disjoined limbs
crawling across
our broken stage.

cringe, as they
lick their lips.

Madame Mercury's Traveling Creepshow: Ringmaster

come one,
come all.

feast your eyes
upon our
matriarch,
Madame Mercury.
mistress of
the macabre —
murderous, and
morbidly maimed.

see the
suckled
sacrilegious
ringmaster
use her stained snout
to sniff out
your pathetic
painted grins.

watch her
sacrifice scouted souls to
Satan, scrubbing off her
own sins
with their blood.
witness her foxtail flick,
as she rips
apart embalmed epidermis —

she feeds
on your fears.

Root Canal

my love for you is thick, golden brown,
colored like smeared layers of caky foundation.
my love for you is crisp, tangy, sour as lemon drops
and limes on cocktail's edge.
my love for you is sharp, brutal,
piercing the flesh of bodies like rusty nails to a cross.

love like this is nocturnal.
love like this kills its characters.
love like this rips and pulls, drags
its fangs along fraying seams.

love like that poisons, spreads same as
arsenic seen under fluorescent lights.
love like that smears paint across canvas,
sparing your parts for pigment.
love like that peers through blinds;
it prays you can't see it pant.

love like mine is bent,
twisted around arms like white sheets.
love like mine is electric,
murdering mosquitoes for comfort.
love like mine is needles,
filing down pupils.

but love like yours,
love like yours is mutilating,
it pulls teeth
to make its own smile.

I See Dead People
Hannah Ross

Dee Richards

Why I Don't Write Poetry

He said: "Stop being so depressing; you'll never get a boyfriend
that way!"
She said: "I looked a lot better at your age."
They said: "You'd be a lot prettier if you smiled more."
Yet, here we are.

Casey Jones

Edward Supranowicz

Hannah Ross

Awaited

The Chief —
a weatherman
plotted patterns,
watched tested waters,
and staved off storms.

The jukebox —
hummed of home.
A waitress with a red grin,
he flirts for that same
chocolate shake,
taking the prize for his charm.

The cane —
Disguised to be used to assist,
was weaponized on
rambunctious children.
His cackle was heard wickedly.

The car —
Cursing at passersby.
Humming an unknown tune,
one only he knew.
Windows down as he sang,
a voice one couldn't help to
smile to.

Papa

He's become skinny
and frail.
He used to be tall
and a fright.
His beard thick,
and red,
now shaved
and white.

Walking and riding for miles
now not even able to sit himself up.
When seen,
a smile constantly covered his lips
but now nothing
but a sneer
or grimace is there.

Why has his brain betrayed him?
To tear away his personality.
The quirks he possessed,
The jokes he told,
The life he lived,
The people he loved.
No longer remembered.

It's killing him.
And I'm watching it do the murdering.
Over
and over
and over
again.

Full Moon
Bella Van Tassel

Jimmy Gallegos Snyder

North East by Eight East/West Lanes

One-zero-six South Butterfield Road was a yellow
house with a red brick front. One hundred
yards from eight east/west lanes of Interstate
Ten. Cigarettes and baseball on a
black and white TV crackle into the floor. The room in the north/east
corner shared a last gasp with its latest inhabitant.
Ice cubes tinkle scotch glasses, "cheers," clinking. This
time, next year, he would be passed, skin as yellow as the nicotine
they would scrub from the walls. As yellow as the house with a red brick front.
Only a cigarette burn, upon the golden carpet, to mark his time in that place.
A little boy in the hallway. Certain that he once saw him there.

One hundred yards from eight east/west lanes of Interstate
Ten, like a hospital room now, painted yellow, it matches
the whites of an old woman's eyes.
They trace the faces, there to say goodbye.
"Gracias Abuelita."
"Ve con Dios mama."
For their lives and lifetimes. She wears an expression
not unlike the bust of the Sacred Heart of Christ sitting alone on a dresser top.
Thorns. Tears of blood.
She carries the old world away with her.
A little boy in the hallway watches her go.

One hundred yards from eight east/west lanes of Interstate
Ten, a room with white walls, a dresser with a turntable on top.
A twin bed, ceiling fan, a black cat pulls
its claws from the golden carpet. There's a cigarette burn
where a little boy builds with LEGOs.
No longer a kid in the hall, this is his room now. This is
his space in this place. He only shares it with ghosts

who sound like eight east/west lanes of Interstate Ten.
One hundred yards from the north/east room of the
house, the yellow house with a red brick front, at
one-zero-six South Butterfield Road.

Thirty Skins a Night

Learning to cover a song is
like climbing into another person's skin.

You begin on the acoustic guitar,
perhaps you will not play that instrument later.
Study the structure, the skeleton.
Hard bone and cartilage for you to suck on.
Don't chew. Suck. And you will,
really bad, until you chart the osteology.
then, suddenly, it blooms in you.

Next hear the heartbeat.
Thump it with your thumb on the body of
your guitar. Strands of melody,
like muscle fiber, strung together
vibrations in the places where ligament attaches
tissue to bone. Harmony in concert with heartbeat.

Sing the suit of skin onto your body. Play it back
to the source with your own interpretations,
of course. The words are not your own.
But you've grown into them.
Intimately.

Change skins thirty times in a night.
Now you're the front man in a cover band.
And a shaman.

It Comes Out at Night

Bella Van Tassel

Talahni Turpin

I Praise…

I praise the black braids
where I can still feel the comb
gliding into my scalp like ice skates.
I praise the black braids
that sits in a box shape
like the almighty Cleopatra.
I praise the black braids
that hangs with pink and yellow colorful beads
that brings an innocent smile
to the little girl's cheeks.
I praise the black braids
with their embedded shapes
on the back of their heads
that would guide the fellow ancestors
when they were lost on their journey.

I praise the kinky hair
how each strand spirals and bounces
up and down with admiration.
I praise the kinky hair how the smells
of tropical coconuts and shea butters
aromes throughout the room.
I praise the kinky hair: in a sweet bun, standing tall and firm like a pineapple.
I praise the kinky hair
how when it's brushed out
it can stretch and reach the entire universe.

I praise the wig-- I can slap it on my head when I go out.
I praise the wig when I want to be somebody else
curly, straight, or even a short cotton candy bob.
I praise the wig
because there is not one type of wig.
I praise black hair
because there are no limitations
what it can or cannot do.

Ripped Me in Two
Bella Van Tassel

Ingrid Yoxsimer

Love Language No. 6: Performative Cruelty

He throws his hands in the air
like he's preaching and lights up again,
rocking back and forth
And back and forth, like the swing of a censer,
full of sacred incense and smoke.

I am but a spectator
to the magnificent show of his being
A single part of the congregation
that holds onto his every breath with both hands,
like it is their own last gasp of life.

He teaches me how to break hearts
As a ritual, as if we're breaking bread.
And I feel him feast on my own as an example,
As if it were the first meal of his life.

Starving, he devours me,
and whispers prayers, syrupy and sweet.
Dripping from his sugared lips to my ear,
to both sides of my brain, until I say
his name like I'm saying Amen.

And I begin to understand,
The ***language of politics is the language of love***
And it is his mother tongue.

Love Poem

holding back your hair, in bathroom stalls,
I love you with the quiet reverence of knees on holy tile.
Sharpie scripture on the sweating halfway walls,
two letters in a heart, they read as a protest and a prayer.
I love you as a child in utero, as a widow in mourning,
and like a soldier loves God in a foxhole,
I love you as a forest loves the fire that consumes it,
and as a mother loves the bump below her ribs.
I love you like a man who has never seen the coast
stares at the sandy calendar page for July.
And sometimes it is too much,
water screaming in a kettle,
the methodic creak of a rocking chair.
too earnest, too stubborn, too much.

the last bell before summer,
the sound of you in a bathroom stall
with a quiet reverence, in these Sharpie scripture walls,
this is how I love you.

FEATURED ARTIST

Self Portrait

In Cemento Veritas

Mario Loprete
Catanzaro, Italy 1968

Painting for me is the first love. An important, pure love. Creating a painting, starting from the spasmodic research of a concept with which I want to send a message to transmit my message, it's the base of my painting. The sculpture is my lover, my artistic betrayal to the painting. That voluptuous and sensual lover that gives me different emotions, that touched prohibited cords…

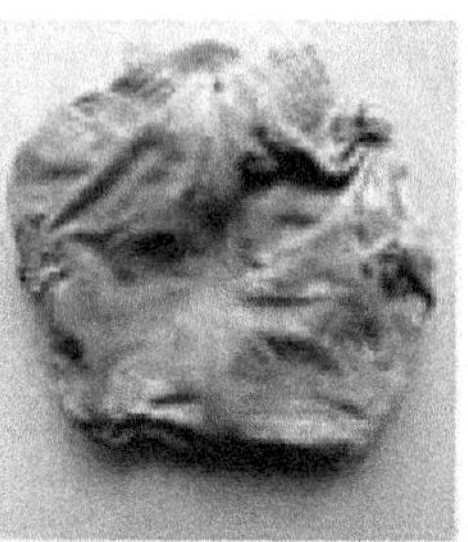

Concrete Sculpture

Concrete Sculpture

Club Dogo
Oil on Concrete

Fabri Fibra
Oil on Concrete

Fabri Fibra
Oil on Concrete

J-Ax

Oil on Concrete

Pharrell
Oil on Concrete

PROSE

Elizabeth Aguilar

Counting Pennies

Both of the foal's frail front legs had already crowned, and the mare was trying everything she could to ease him from her body. Rolling to-and-fro on the ground, standing up and laying down, but he seemed to be stuck at the shoulders, a sign of real trouble. Kelli had seen her father handle dystocia once before but never imagined she would be repositioning an unborn foal herself, in the forest of all places, an hour away from any help of course. The mare had been in labor for over a half-hour, and it was getting riskier with every additional minute that was lost. Air supply is critical, and there would be permanent brain damage or worse if she labored much longer. If this foal didn't make his way out in the next fifteen minutes, there would likely be no hope left to hold onto.

Kelli tries to soothe the mare, "Penny," stroking the contracting mound of belly that lies before her, but it is useless, she is too panicked. Penny had been straining for far too long, and the look in her eyes is one of growing desperation.

Ten minutes left.

Kelli makes sure to keep a trailing fingertip on Penny as she makes her way around. She gently reaches for one of the foal's extended legs and cups the tiny hoof in her hand for a moment. She knows what needs to be done. Placing a reassuring hand on Penny, she summons her inner strength, and uses her fingers to trail the foal's leg all the way inside to his chest. Kelli gives him a gentle push back, and retreats; then takes the other front leg and gently pulls it forward, carefully timing with Penny's contractions and cries.

Five minutes left.

"Okay girl, you got it now!" she pleads hopefully.

Kelli backs away, trudging into the soft snow that borders the clearing in which they had found refuge. As Penny's powerful contractions move like waves through her body, Kelli feels helpless. She's done everything she knows to help, and all she can do now is wait.

With his shoulders unsquared, and some effort on Penny's part, the foal is finally freed. Penny and the foal lay apart in exhaustion for a moment. It is over. Penny turns her head back to her baby, meeting him for the first time — and what a moving moment it is. He teeters in wobbly motions as his first breaths create the tiniest of clouds that escape into the crisp air; he's beautiful It is then that Kelli knows she has to leave them here. The only question remaining in her mind is, how the hell is she going to explain this back at home? Her family might not have noticed her extended absence, but they will surely notice the blood stained on her fresh jeans.

After the ride back, Kelli sat in her car beside the frosted barn. It was just across the way from the two-story farmhouse she had lived in since she was three, all the way at the end of S. Marybelle Ave; a dirt road that divided the vast surrounding farmlands. Kelli's stone-like expression masked the frenzy of thoughts that were rambling inside her mind; they mimicked the erratic chugging of her idling engine. The only sign of life from the car were clouds of breath escaping through the crack of her window.

Emerging from foggy thoughts, her eyes refocus to find her delicate hands resting on the steering wheel. Her nails are unpainted and lined with grime, and her fingers are fiddling with one of the many old skeleton keys she had hunted for around town at various garage sales. This one was special though; it had held its ground in her pocket through all the madness of today.

After kicking off her boots, worn with daily abuse, she brushes past a wood-planked wall lined with denim jackets and boots that smell of cow fields, a nostalgic smell. She makes her way down the hallway but stops at the monument of her achievements her mother had arranged long ago. It showcased a blue ribbon for horsemanship, an "Outstanding Citizen" award for her hours volunteered at the animal shelter, and a gold-tipped trophy for placing in the county barrel-racing contest. Just like her mother, Kelli had a passion for animals— and the patience for horses. She had always aspired to be a rodeo-veterinarian for the South Dakota Rodeo circuit but could never seem to scrape together the funds for classes. More important things always seemed to take precedence; first there were roots in the plumbing, then the electrical panel surged, then the water heater busted…it was always something. When something went awry, everyone's contributions were vital, which left little room for Kelli's dreams. However, she took great care to learn all she could through her experiences on the family ranch, and always did as she was told.

Kelli must have been gone longer than she realized because the kitchen wasn't bustling with boys like it usually was, it looked like a ghost town with dirty plates and silverware left scattered across the table and counters. The only one who had not already gone to bed was Grandpa Chach, who was cleaning up the aftermath of the sloppy frenzy they called supper.

"Well hey there darlin', I've got dinner ready for— *Oh Jesus Kelli, are you hurt*??"

"No Grandpa, I'm just fine."

"Well what in the hell happened? There's blood stains all on your new denims!"

"Well, ya know Penny, that pregnant wild mare cousin Lou gave us because she kept runnin' off?"

"Did she bite you up? I *told* your daddy she was a wild one."

"No sir. I went out to feed her and noticed she was actin' real peaked-like, so I went and mixed her up some honey and oats. When I came back and opened her gate, she bolted! I hopped in my truck and tracked her for ages 'til I found her miles away, breathing all heavy on the ground beneath a big ol' pine. I looked in her eyes and she seemed real scared, then I noticed little legs comin' from her other end."

"Oh shit!" Grandpa gasped. "Ya hear of mares puttin' off their labor 'til nobody's watchin,' but *that's* ridiculous. She's a tough one for sure."

"Yessir. I was real scared too, but I didn't let her know that. I could tell somethin' was wrong 'cuz she was pushin' and pushin' but nothing was happening, so I went right in there and turned that baby 'round, just like you taught me."

"Oh you did, did you?"

"Yessir. I stayed on her the whole time to make sure the foal came out alright."

"Well that's good dear, who would've thought Lou's screw-ups would actually pay off for once! So did they settle into the barn okay?"

"Well Grandpa, I know she could've hauled our plow, and her foal might've fetched us a little extra at auction…but I think if she kept running off because she wanted to raise her baby in the forest so bad, then we oughta let her."

Grandpa Chach ceased drying the dish in his hand. His gaze flew across the kitchen and straight into Kelli's as he said, "Now, little miss Kelli, that's about the dumbest thing you've ever done.

We're barely scrapin' by and you're lettin' the livestock loose?! Brand new denims don't just fall from the sky you know!" Grandpa Chach turned away in a fury, violently clanking soapy dishes in the sink, trying unsuccessfully to hide his growing distain.

Kelli stands frozen in place as the events of the day replay in her head. As obedient as Kelli normally was, she can't help but lovingly hold her memory of the new mother mare nestled in the dry foliage under the pine tree, nuzzling her newborn behind the cascading veil of delicate snowflakes. To Kelli, it feels like a scene that would be simply immoral to disturb. Before she drove away, she had stolen one last look into the grateful eyes of the liberated mother who had risked everything for the freedom of her newborn child.

Kelli leaves the kitchen defeated by the disappointment of her Grandfather; she knows she will be sent to bed with a rumble in her belly tonight. When she reaches the stairway though, she takes a few extra steps toward her monument once more. Kelli fishes her special key out of her dirty jeans and gently places it on the shelf amongst her other relics of accomplishment. She whispers to herself, "Your mama would have been proud of you today, little miss Kelli," and goes off to bed.

Busiest Bee
Daniel Vidri

Calleigh Backrak

Earth Invaders

"Penelope! Get back in this house this instance, girl! Where do you think you goin' with all that crap on your face?!"

Penny's mama yelled from the porch of their country home. It was just about dusk, and the amber sunlight made everything appear golden.

"Mama, I'll be home by ten!" Penny's cherry red lips matched Vincent's red '62 firebird convertible. She giggled as she hopped into the passenger seat. Vincent was handsome as ever in a black leather jacket, his brunette hair combed back with grease, except for a lock of hair that curled right above his eyebrow. His brown eyes were locked on Penny, a red ribbon tied up her blonde hair.

"Penelope! Penelope! Who is that man?!" Mama hollered.

As Penny was fixing her light blue poodle skirt, Vincent reached over and snuck a kiss.

"Vincent! My mama is right there!"

"Oh yeah, I must've lost my manners—hello, mama!" Vincent flashed a big beautiful smile to mama and waved. Mama whipped the rag in her hand as if to shoo them away, and then she proceeded to stomp back into the house. He skidded out of her gravel driveway, rocks flying. Penny let out a victorious hoot and threw her hands up into the air as they made their way to the Drive-In theatre.

Once they arrived at the Drive-In theatre, Vincent bought two tickets for, *Earth Invaders,* some flick about an alien invasion. He parked his car towards the back of the gravel parking lot. Vincent and Penny held each other tight as they watched the aliens on the silver screen rage havoc on the people of earth. Penny cringed and clung onto Vincent.

"C'mon Penny, it's not that scary."

"Oh Vincent, I know it's not real, but I'm so frightened!"

"You know I'll protect you from anything, baby." They looked deep into one another's eyes and started a long kiss—

Suddenly, a blinding white light interrupted their kiss, and it seemed to surround only Vincent's car. He looked up, keeping a hand over his blinking eyes and roared,

"HEY! TURN OFF THAT DAMN LIGHT!" The whole car started to jolt, and they realized they were being lifted into the big white light above them.

"HELP! SOMEONE HELP!" Penny screamed to the people below them. It was in vain—it seemed that they could not hear her—their faces locked on the aliens of the silver screen.

"I'm getting the hell out of here!" Vincent jumped out of the car and hit the gravel with a hard flop.

"VINCENT! VINCENT! HELP ME!" Penny screamed as Vincent watched his beloved car and his girl get sucked into a white abyss. In the blink of an eye, the white light had vanished.

He found himself gasping and blinking wide eyed at the stars above him. A red ribbon gently fell out of the sky and landed into his palm, —and that was all that remained of his sweet girl, Penny.

Caged Eagle
Daniel Vidri

Tasha Bonsignore

Devil Wind

Paddling to the surface of a deep night's dream, I sense scratchy eyes, cracked lips, and the beginnings of a headache. In the bathroom mirror there's a trickle of blood emerging from my bottom lip and snaking down my neck. Also visible is the reflection of the window behind me, exposing a cold purple dead fisheye sun, shrouded in brown sludge. My cell rings,

"Hi love, I'm here, just waiting for baggage."

"How was the flight babe?" I enquire.

"Oh…was fine. Just the one stopover for TWO HOURS! So annoying. Feeling kinda tired now. Hey, how is everything?"

"It's good. Just got up. So freaking dry here. Gonna shower, then slather myself in body lotion."

"Ok honey, I see my bags. Gotta go. I'll call you when I get to the hotel."

"Sounds good. Love you. Be safe."

"You too. Talk soon."

Why so thirsty? Orange juice? Open the fridge. It's dark. Damn! Musta tripped a circuit breaker. Go to laundry room and open electrical panel. The switches are all in their places. What? The meter dial is not spinning. The power is off again. Call the power company. Ring, Ring, Ring. Wait, Wait, Wait.

"We value your call, please wait until the next representative is available."

I'm thinking all that expensive meat and fish in the freezer could spoil.

"How long will the power be off?"

"We're sorry. We have an indeterminate cause for your area. Please leave your number and we will notify you when we have more information."

Damn! They won't call back! My head is pounding. Why is the air so dry? I suddenly miss the warm mugginess of D.C. Even though the crime was escalating, moving to California had been a bad idea all the way around. The astronomical housing prices, gas prices, taxes, and Jason is always flying off to the Capital for his top secret government meetings. I only see my friends on social media. Look how they are so enjoying life. I'm stuck here in the hills above L.A., in a freeze-dried McMansion, shriveling up like a prune, and my nearest neighbor, whom I've never met, lives in a McCastle surrounded by a prison wall.

I keep flipping on light switches, forgetting that the power is off. So dark, I stub my toe on the claw foot sofa. I open the curtains and blinds; let the light flow in. The sun is now a glaring red Eye of Horus, beaming his piercing gaze across the pool and deck, directly into my soul.

Wait! Why are those mountains moving…and growing? Rub my eyes and look again. There is a beautiful golden outline of the distant hills, with fog or smog rising up and glowing to the south. Where is my cell? I must photograph this unique phenomenon and send it to Jase. Open my phone and I am faced with a:

"Breaking News Alert! The Santana Fire has now scorched 16,000 acres and is 0% contained. Evacuation orders are increased as fierce winds worsen blazes in North Los Angeles County."

I drop the phone in horror. The golden oranges and purples in the hills are fires! Yes, I can see them now, rising up and falling back, like thin bony red-hot fingers, erupting from the earth and clawing at the sky.

Clang, Bing, Bong! What is that infernal noise? Opening the sliding glass door to the pool, a hot dragon's breath hits me with unexpected violence. Patio furniture blown apart, cushions, a lawn chair and barbeque tongs are floating in the pool. The wind chimes have tangled in a tree and jangle in irritation. I quickly slide the door shut on the blast furnace.

What to do? Call Jase. Immediately I'm sent to voice mail.

"Oh My God Jase! It's so hot and windy. There's fire! It's on the ridge. Flames! Please call me when you get this."

What to do? Turn on the TV. Damn remote not working. Needs batteries. Paw around in the "what not" drawer in the kitchen for two freaking AA batteries. Eject old and insert new batteries, aim remote at TV like a loaded pistol. Still no picture. Oh God! How stupid am I? The power is fracking OFF! My hands are shaking. Groping around the floor for my cell I grasp it and scroll through the news.

"Santa Anas from 45 MPH to 100 MPH, hurricane force winds. -- Caution there's an overturned 18-wheeler on the freeway, blown over by strong winds. -- Santa Ana winds carrying hot embers, have sparked numerous smaller fires beyond the main fire. --This Santa Ana meteorological phenomenon is causing the lowest relative humidity levels ever recorded in L.A County."

Santa Ana! What in hells name is a Santa Ana? My head is throbbing, can't think, my split lip has formed a crimson lightning streak of blood down the front of my crème blouse. I continue scrolling down: here's a video of a young blonde woman in wide eyed alarm.

"…It was like a tornado, honestly, it was so windy, and so much smoke…I just ran through it."

"And now we go live on the scene to Ridgetop Bluff in the North of the County. Are you there Zach? Zach nods, in his fire jacket, suspender pants and helmet, face mask dangling around his neck, sirens and flashing lights in the distance.

"I'm here in the Huntington Hills subdivision at the Bluff. As you can see, a lot of smoke here. The crews are still battling blazes two streets south of here. One couple survived the flames that suddenly engulfed their home, by diving into the backyard swimming pool, and using snorkels to breathe."

The camera pans to a black lagoon of ash, with lawn furniture jutting out of the water, amid a faux Romanesque pool surrounded by toppled burnt columns, looking like the last days of Pompeii.

Zach continues, "…the couple is now at Cedars-Sinai Medical Center receiving treatment for smoke inhalation, their condition is unknown at this time. Back to you Stephen…"

But Stephen has disappeared. The screen is dark and the phone needs recharging. I toss the phone aside, there's no power to charge it. I walk to the patio door and place my trembling hands on the glass. The smell is startlingly pungent, like the campfires at the cabin. I recall singing songs and roasting marshmallows, the warm crispy chocolatey crunch of a s'more. The crackle and popping of the fire. The laughter. I remember a movie about Hiroshima. The victims of the nuclear bomb who wore black colored clothes, absorbed more radioactive heat than those who had worn light colored clothes. One person who had been wearing a black and white striped shirt, had striped burn marks across his back.

Slowly, I go to my closet and remove my bloodstained blouse and black slacks. I put on a white terry cloth bathrobe and pour a glass of Chardonnay. Breathing in the campfire scented air, I feel those good memories loosen my tight neck and shoulder muscles.

While sipping the fine wine, I savor the sting of alcohol on my dry split lips and contemplate a cool dip in the pool.

Everyone Hates You

The acoustic earmuffs did not protect my heart from the guilt of the havoc and devastation I was wreaking. We used chain saws, pole saws, a larger and smaller bobcat, and a huge truck with a wood chipper attached out the back into which we constantly dragged branches and vegetation of all kinds, and shoved them into the hellaciously noisy masticator which devoured greenery like a starved dragon. The tall proud saguaros and tropical hibiscus, the juicy succulents and jasmine in bloom, riotous red and pink papery bougainvillea blossoms swirling like a magenta tornado, all sucked into the greedy maw. Acacia, yucca, pepper trees both Brazilian and Californian, all disappeared as if they had never grown there at all, leaving a very long, 500-foot by 7-foot corridor of dirt and sawdust. And the reason for this wanton destruction of a peaceful leafy haven of green? This was the path I intended to follow to install the sewer line from my house to the manhole, completely on my property.

The crazy thing about the configuration of the shape of my land was that I owned not a square, or rectangular, or even a flag shaped lot, but more of a lamp post shape; a large main block of land with a broad 150 foot by 20 foot band to the east, and then a skinny long 870 foot by 7 foot strip to the south. The skinny strip bordered at least 10 other properties like a disobedient, ungovernable territory, willfully detached from the mother ship and stabbing all neighboring land like a probing ice pick, all sharpened and looking for trouble.

Being a new transplant to the staid, respectable and traditional lane on Mt. Helix, I trod ever so lightly the first twelve months on my terra firma, mostly tending to the CPR of the dilapidated 85-year-old structure called a "house." The roof leaked, a bedroom ceiling had fallen in, a sliding door would close but not reopen, trapping the unwary victim in a paint peeling room with no light switch. So much to scrape and sand and caulk and repair, and prime and paint. I started before sunup and fell into bone weary oblivion at sundown. But when the bathroom slowly developed its own opinion on just when it would allow a flush – or not, I realized the ancient septic system was acting in accordance with her age and notifying us that she be laid to rest.

Upon discovering that there was no room to install a new onsite treatment system because it would have to be 100 feet away from the well, I got out my maps, rulers, and the grant deed to determine if the great leap from septic to sewer was even possible. Was my skinny troublesome ice pick near enough to a manhole to allow a sewer line access? I went on an exploratory walk through the jungle I owned but had not traversed and caught the glint of angry eyes peering at me through the shrubbery. "What are you doing here?" "This is our property!" "You are trespassing!" The psychiatrist and his Gladys Kravitz doppelganger wife got right up in my face and said "…this is our property, we paid one thousand dollars to have it surveyed, so get off our land and… EVERYONE HATES YOU."

When I was the new kid at La Mesa Elementary School, there was a ripe crop of mean girls running the playground. One girl would hold up my braids and yell "run horsey" and use my hair as the reins. If I turned to face her, she would pull my hair hard, and her friends would push me forward. I was their horse. When they found out that I told the principal about their horsey game they didn't touch me but threw my lunch bag into the trash and taunted me with the primary school sing song tune… "EVERYBODY HATES YOU."

Since the beginning of humanity, wars over territorial domination have been fought and won, and lost, over and over. Some social historians and anthropologists have postulated that humans are evolutionarily hard wired with a territorial imperative. We are endowed with an innate instinct toward property ownership and nation building. There's a persistent human drive to acquire land and defend territory. Wasn't it our old poet friend Robert Frost who proclaimed, "Good fences make good neighbors?"

But the woman who had planted and tended this foliage and greenery was desolate. These were her babies, her children, and I had killed them all. She held her abdomen and rocked back and forth making a keening sound. All of her offspring had been cut off at their shins and laid in tangled piles of elbows and knees. And yet she was not informed by the landowner; "Hey honey, don't plant your beauties on that skinny strip of land, because I don't own it and there may come a day of reckoning. But maybe he felt insulated and safe. He owned that place for thirty years and no one ever invaded the unruly strip bordering his piece, or ever bothered him about it. Thirty years is a long time and people get comfortable in their ignorance.

So after many polite but to the point letters to the affected neighbors, and the lawyer's letters to them when they ignored mine, by not allowing my territorial imperative on the land they thought was their own, but in fact was not, and after the surveyors completed their extensive record of survey on my lamp post shaped property, and the County voted to allow my annexation into the neighboring sewer district, and the water district extracted their pound of flesh, the trench digging heavy machinery is slated to arrive next week. The dust will fly, and the noise will be unbearable at times as the clanking metal dinosaurs bite down, down, six feet down into the earth grabbing roots and dragging them up into the sunlight, clutching them in steel jaws and shaking them to death, then stacking them into a barbed and spiky mound to be carted to a land fill.

This is the way humans dominate the land. This is the way landowners anger their neighbors, and this is the way to make everyone hate you.

Old Rebel
Daniel Vidri

Beth Ferris

Mercy

Arborville, USA was once a thriving farming community. After the petro-tank crashed into the main irrigation ditch, fouling the water beyond purification, the farmland became a wasteland in a matter of months, never to recover. All that is left is the central thoroughfare with a strip mall of dilapidated buildings and a scattering of old farmhouses that would make the American Pickers salivate if invited to dig through their hidden treasures.

Maine Street is now dusty and barren; the remaining population, pale withered wraiths silently passing, without conversation or awareness of their surroundings. Their lives had become a mundane existence driving to and from the envelope factory in the next county. Suddenly, a series of short, sharp explosions, reverberate throughout the silent town causing the towns peoples' heads to turn in unison like a herd of deer suddenly sensing a hunter's presence. The realization that the noise is only the backfire of an ancient stake-bed Ford does not relieve them of their trepidation; if anything, it has increased it. Everywhere, people are quickly retreating indoors to the safety it offers.

The truck belongs to Azurah Hamshel, the town's requisite mean-old-man, affectionately known as Pain in the Az, minus the affection. He recklessly pulls in front of the general store stopping with a screech of rusty brakes. His eyes glance up and down the street, seeking a fight from any, but are soon disappointed. By the time he gains the steps, the street is vacant of human life. He climbs the stairs; slams open the door and clomps into the darkened interior.

The proprietor, a mousy man, hides behind the counter, wiping sweat from his shiny bald pallet. Az says nothing, he merely raises his head, his eyes becoming visible under the brim of his thinning straw hat. Those bright blue eyes are red-rimmed with a malice that is notorious throughout the county. The proprietor, now shaking with fear, pushes a paper bag full of groceries across the counter. Az grabs the bag, turns around and leaves. The proprietor does not ask the angry man for payment, he is simply relieved to have avoided Az's scathing temper one more time. He knew Az would send him a check through the mail at the end of the month.

None of the residents of Arborville remember Azurah as a young man, full of hope and vigor. He has always been known as Az, even before the poisoning of their farmlands; a man whose legendary ire scared even the staunchest of his surviving neighbors. He was one of the few to stubbornly refuse to sell his ruined land. His old rickety home, the only structure still standing, the barn long since lost to a lightning strike several decades earlier.

As reputations go, Az's was well earned. There was not a fight he would back down from. Ask old Henry, the drunk, who made the mistake of denting Az's truck on one of his weekly grocery runs. Az slashed every tire and threatened, in a gravelly voice,

"Tell the sheriff, you be the next to get a slashing" as he slides his finger across his throat to make his meaning quite clear.

Even the packs of violent, migrant crop workers who regularly passed through to the next farm town knew better than to rouse Az's anger. The last confrontation ended up with three of the five in the hospital with broken bones and bloodied faces, none of them willing to point a finger at Az knowing full well he would track them down and break every single tattling digit.

Az slides into the rut that serves as a driveway to what is left of his farm, a cloud of dirt and gravel rattling against the front porch of his house. Just past the driveway, off the side of the main road, a faded truck is haphazardly parked. At the back of the truck, a group of teenagers dressed in ratty t-shirts and holey jeans, gather around the tailgate poking and prodding at a burlap sack that thrashes with every insult. Az leaves his truck, eyeing the boys as he takes his groceries inside. He comes back out and stands on the porch staring at the intruders, not recognizing them. He pulls on his raggedy beard, deciding just how annoying their presence in close proximity to his home was becoming to his bitter sensibilities.

Suddenly, the woeful howl of a cat as she is pulled from the burlap sack by her tail, rends the air. Az is moving before he even realizes it, heading straight for the truck and the unaware men. Az is less than a few feet away, when one of the men looks up and realizes their peril. His eyes widen in alarm, as he backs away towards the cab of the truck, pulling at the other men, trying to warn them as well. He is unsuccessful.

Az advances towards the other men, their backs still facing him, when he grabs the closest neck, pinching it so forcibly that the man withers to the ground, unable to move. The remaining two men look up, noticing their friend's sudden absence, and flinch back when they recognize Az's furious face. His whipcord-muscled arms strike out to both sides, knocking the remaining men back with sudden force. The men fall to the ground, rolling with the momentum and gain their feet in a fluid response. The man to go to ground first, having inched away in the dirt unnoticed, stood as well. The men barely glance back at Az before scrambling into the cab of the truck.

There is a moment's delay, enough time for Az to reach up and pull the terrified cat into his sheltering arms, before the truck fires to life, tires spinning, and races away showering Az in a billow reddened soil. Az looks on, noting the men and the truck for future torments.

Az carries the cat inside and sets her gently down on the floor in the kitchen. He reaches into the pantry, dumps out dried potatoes from a box, and then grabs a thread-bare blanket which he shakes out before placing in the box. Using the tip of his foot, he slowly scooches the box next to the cat so as to not startle her. He turns away, looking for a bowl to which he ladles a spoonful of stew from the cold pot of last night's dinner and places it on the ground next to the box. He leaves the kitchen without looking at the cat and goes out to the porch, sitting down in a rickety chair barely held together with old strips of cracked leather. There is a look of utter bewilderment on Az's face.

He absently scratches at the band-aide in the crook of his right arm; a memento of yesterday's visit to the dialysis clinic in the city. His kidneys had been failing for years. This monthly purge was just another insult to injury; an ongoing torment that would only prolong his miserable life for a little bit longer. He shakes his head as if to pry loose the memory that briefly flared to life when he heard the cat's pitiful cry, but his attempts to remember are unsuccessful; the memory is just too painful for him to consciously revisit. He tilts his head back and closes his eyes; sleep comes to him unexpectedly.

Az dreams. The light brightens slowly, bringing into focus a small room. The first thing he sees is the hand-carved bed Az had made as a wedding gift for his new bride. In the corner, the light still hazy, is the cradle he and his wife built together when they discovered they were going to be parents. In the bed is his lovely wife, still flushed from the exertions of labor. Her auburn hair cascades down her left shoulder, leaving the right shoulder uncovered for the nursing infant snuggled into his mother's bare breast. His wife looks up at him, her eyes shining with love and trust. Azurah falls to his knees, tears cascading down his face as emotions fill him to bursting; it has been half a century since he had felt this joy.

His wife's scream shatters his great rapture. It is a cry of overwhelming pain and anguish, just like the young cat's. The room darkens with a single narrow beam focusing on his wife who stands over the cradle, hunched, as she takes great handfuls of hair and pulls. In the cradle, the sight of his son, now blue in death, unhinges him from his sanity. It is a place that not even his wife's love can retrieve him from. Only hate and anger can pierce this miasma of grief and guilt that Az has fallen into. This rage that shaped his life from then on.

In his unconscious state, Az shudders with the pain of remembering. He is unaware when the cat slips on silent feet into his lap and begins to quietly hum. Within Az's broken mind, a feminine voice speaks to him, "You are not responsible for your child's death. Why do you still carry this burden?" Az has no answer for her. So much time has passed since that moment in his life; he has forgotten the why of that burden, only that the pain was too much to relive.

"Do you want to live old man?" the voice asks him.

He considers her question, was death better than the kind of life he was living? If that were so, then why hadn't he let himself die years ago when he was diagnosed with kidney failure? A bottle of rock gut would have ended him in a matter of days. Az, fearing the unknown more than this misery, and with monumental stubbornness that has kept him alive, he tells the voice in his head,

"No, I don't wanna to die today".

"Then you will not, but you must let go of this grief and anger, they no longer serve any purpose but to poison the life you have left. Can you do that old man?" He nods his head in compliance.

Hours later, Azurah slowly wakens. The constant pain in his back from his failing kidneys is gone. He remembers his wife and son; it still hurts, these memories, but the pain is bearable.

There is no sign of the cat, save for an empty box and a half-eaten bowl of cold stew on the floor of his kitchen.

Payback's a Bitch, or in This Case, a Demon

I opened my mailbox in a hurry to get my paycheck and cash it for tonight's date with Shelby. From within, little slivers of paper wafted in the air and deliberately drifted to the ground; I couldn't wrap my mind around what I was seeing. I gave my mailbox another hard look, half-full of shredded paper; confettied despair slowly emp tied as if it was being pushed out from within. In my mind, I could hear its vicious laughter pounding against the back of my eyes. I would have to cancel my date with Shelby, again. This was not the first time this f'n mailbox had interfered with my social life. I nearly lost my job last month when my boss had mailed me a business portfolio for me to review while he was out of town. How do I explain to him that it was accidently-on-purpose shredded in a cursed mailbox?

There are some people in the world that you just don't piss off. For me, it was the Jamaican mail lady. I don't' even remember how it all started other than a vague memory of harassing her because she was taking too long to fill the boxes and refused to let anyone get their mail until she was finished with her job. One day I opened up my mailbox to find a small crudely made figure, of burlap and course leather, its face painted black, eyes and mouth outlined in white in the expression of a petulant child, the body was shaped like an animal with twisted limbs and a fat scaly tail that I could not identify. There was no mistaking the dark malevolence radiating from its gleaming ruby irises. I had no doubt who had put it there. Jamaicans are well known for their arcane lore as part of their culture passed down through the generations, as well as having no compunction about using it, whether white or black magic.

As I reached in to pull the evil thing out, I let out a pathetic yelp before jerking my hand back as a sharp pain starting at my fingertip, radiated across my hand and up my arm. The single glistening blood drop poised on its head slowly disappeared as it was absorbed, then the whole thing disintegrated into a pile of ash. Ignorant as I was of black magic, I knew this was very, very bad.

The fact of being cursed didn't sink in at first. Having my mail delivered to another tenant's box was nothing out of the ordinary in a complex that housed almost 200 tenants. However, when my box number started moving around to different locations in the mailroom, I started to pay attention. Outgoing mail was instantly transported back to my mailbox, even if I used an off-sight location. I even tried renting a post office box and forwarding my mail; the mail always came back to my box in the complex. I knew I was in trouble when an oversized package I was expecting ended up crammed into my box. It took me days to pry the package out, piece by piece, evil laughter echoing in my head the whole time.

Next, I tried searching the internet for "how to break a curse" under the white magic sites. This site looked promising:

> **Are You Really Cursed?**
>
> Be sure to read the Magical Self-Defense article before you continue on this one because it
>
> does detail ways to determine if you are, in fact, under magical attack. In general, though, you
>
> should be able to answer *all three* of the following questions with a yes:
>
> Is there someone in your life that you have angered or offended in some way?
>
> Is that person someone who has the magical knowledge to place a harmful spell on you?
>
> Is a hex or curse the only possible explanation for what is happening to you?

Yep. That would be me. Now what? The site tells me I need to take protective measures and that there are several ways to do so. The first suggestion was to use a magical mirror to reflect the curse back on the sender, especially useful if you know the identity of the person who cursed you. So, I print up the instructions and follow them to a tee, preparing and then placing the "magic mirror" in the mailbox and repeat my intent several times. Just as the final word echoes through the empty mailroom, there is a loud crack as the mirror suddenly fractures, I have just enough time to duck before the whole thing explodes into a cloud of glass particles and scatters across the floor. The curse was supposed to reflect back on the Jamaican mail lady, instead, on top of my mail being smeared with something very stinky, I had her screaming in my face the very next day. Of course, she wasn't looking so good, had these little sores all over her face.

The next recommendation was to use a protective decoy poppet or magic doll as defensive tool to take the damage in your place. I make the doll, say the words to activate it and place it in the mailbox. No sooner had I set it down, when the damn thing catches fire and burns to a pile of ash in a matter of seconds. Well, that was not helpful, it only served to make the curse worse, with the mail confetti being the first insult; further retaliation involved animal feces.

It was on the third pass of the website that I noticed tiny print at the bottom of the site:

> **Curses or spells involving demons require a different approach. Demons require blood for binding, in order to break the binding spell, the same blood is needed. To find spells to unbind a demon, check our other site on black magic and search for demons.**

Now that I knew there was a way to lift this demonic curse, I just needed to get the Jamaican mail lady's blood. That was the easy part. I placed a piece of tape with metal tacks embedded in it to the door of my mailbox. I had to listen to her scream in my face, again, but she didn't think to retrieve the tape, which had little speckles of her blood all over it. That night, using the spell I printed from the new web site, I lit a black candle, and burned the written spell smeared with the mail lady's blood. Afterwards, I was so tired, I barely made it to bed where I slept without waking till the next afternoon, just in time to wait for the mail delivery. Our previous mail person had been replaced. The new guy told me that the Jamaican was in the hospital and would not be returning.

"Jamaicans and their dark magic…that's what you get when you mess with demons" he said in a dead-pan voice.

"Good to know", I said with a knowing chuckle. I checked my mailbox, opening it slowly, expecting the worst, and when I found nothing amiss with my mail, no shredding, no animal feces, no explosions, I sighed with relief, feeling that these tribulations were finally over.

Just as the new mailman turned away, at the last moment, his eyes, which had been normal human eyes only a moment ago, were now fully black, glittering with a tinge of blood red. His smiled stretched across his face, rows of dagger like teeth flashing briefly for a second.

Still Got It

Daniel Vidri

Rebecca Kanter

Popsicle Gossip in July

Frozen grape concentrate on sticks. She opens the cooler and passes them around to three friends who sunbathe at the community pool. They tear white wrappers and avoid drippy purple slime. *Did you hear what she said the other day?* In the aqua shallows of the stairs, a baby's plump arms splish-splash underneath a floppy cotton hat, which is secured at his chin with a string. Where it's deeper, goggles, floaties, kickboards, and foam noodles jostle the choppy surface. A bee attempts a drink amidst the chaos. *No, what crazy thing did she say now?* The lifeguard's megaphone declares that it's time for the swim test. It's for the brave who want to play on the other side of the candy cane rope, where the black tile lines on the bottom slope down sharply. It's for those who don't mind the aching compression in their ears as they wriggle down to retrieve a sunken ring. *Did she accuse you of causing undue stress again, just because you asked her to pick up the customers' trash? Even though it's clearly in her job description?* A girl with a drippy "s" shaped ponytail runs by, printing puddles on the pavement. The lifeguard's whistle is three short bursts. "Walk!" The girl slows to a skip. Tiny triangle flags strung over the pool yield to the breeze. *She said something even more unbelievable: that we don't work well together because I'm* jealous *of her.* A boy bounds down the undulating diving board, and leaps with wild arms and billowing swim trunks. His belly flop smacks the air. The friends laugh. *If you're jealous of a manipulative faker, then I'm a monkey's uncle.* They laugh again. The footprint puddles are already shrinking off the scorching deck.

Provenance

Madrid, 1898
In a spring garden, with high stucco walls, the artist's boots crunch over steppingstones. "Here are my exquisite daughters." Then the sisters enjoy melon, cured ham, and Rioja wine. They sit on a wooden bench, wearing white dresses, near a napping cat. Generous brush strokes convey merriment and a red carnation tucked behind an ear. Recollections of childhood lead to whispers of a suitor.

Paris, 1956
In a summer dining room, with high doorways, the heiress' ballet flats leave momentary impressions on the carpet. "Here are my grandmother and her sisters." Then the friends enjoy niçoise salad, cigarettes, and sherry. They sit at a mahogany table, wearing Chanel dresses, near a ticking clock. Generous stories convey wartime relations and a portrait tucked inside a closet. Recollections of adolescence lead to whispers of an affair.

London, 1990
In an autumn auction house, with high culture, the collector's wingtips tap the marble floor. "Here is my chance." Then the audience enjoys canapés, Impressionist art, and scotch. Generous bids convey validation of masterworks and hope tucked inside wallets. They sit in folding rows, wearing shoulder-padded suits, near the pounding gavel. Recollections of fraud lead to whispers of warning.

New York, Today
In a winter gallery, with high security, the curator's pumps strike the shiny parquet floor. "Here is one of our new donations." Then the gala guests enjoy bacon-wrapped asparagus, crab cakes, and white wine. They sit on leather benches, wearing cocktail attire, near a performing cellist. Generous contributions convey their appreciation, and the authenticated provenance tucked inside a filing cabinet. Recollections of art history classes lead to whispers that this is one of the artist's finest pieces.

What Do You Have There, Son?

Because there are no seat belts in the front seat of their black Plymouth, the boy's mother uses her arm to keep him from falling forward, as she brakes into a parking spot on First Avenue. She twists her cigarette stub into the ash tray and cranks her window up. The boy follows her down the block, to the bank on the corner. She wears a floral print dress, with a full skirt, narrow belt, and a button-up collar. He wears a striped t-shirt, baggy shorts, socks pulled up to mid-calf, and brown leather shoes. He would rather be riding bikes and throwing rocks at windows with his older brothers, but his mother has taken him on her Saturday morning errands.

Inside the bank, he makes a mental game of counting the squares on the patterned marble floor, as he and his mother make their way to one of the gilded teller cages. He knows he is not to speak a word or leave his mother's side, otherwise it will mean a belt lashing later from his father.

But something catches his eye under the ornate, lamp-lit table that customers use to prepare their deposits. While his mother chats with the teller, he quietly sneaks over. It's a man's gold watch! He looks around. There are no other customers in the bank. He'll have enviable stacks of comic books and Bazooka gum.

"William!" his mother scolds.

He dashes back to her, the watch hidden in his fist.

•

On a Friday evening, the girl's father drives his family to a Mexican restaurant in their yellow Subaru station wagon. He likes to celebrate the end of the work week by splurging some of his paycheck on a nice meal and venting about his boss. As the girl follows her family inside, she pretends that the grout lines on the tile floor are streets of a tiny city.

"Smoking or Non?" the hostess asks.

"Non," her parents reply in unison.

The hostess clutches a stack of menus and leads them to a booth. A bus boy places four red plastic cups of ice water on the table, along with a basket of glistening tortilla chips and a black mortar bowl of salsa.

The girl notices three stained-glass windows. They are each different mosaics of white adobe rancho buildings with red tile roofs, desert sand, prickly pear cacti, and brown mountains.

Her father follows her gaze, then issues his daughters a challenge. “Can you find the coyote in one of those windows?” It takes a minute, but the girl spots him. He is a tiny silhouette, off in the distance, howling on a mountain peak.

After they order, her father says, “Did you know that this building used to be a bank? There was a row of teller windows along that wall.” The girl tries to imagine them. “Once, when I was about your age,” he says, “I found a gold watch. Right over there where those people are sitting.” The girl tries to imagine her father as a boy. “I wanted to keep the watch, of course, but I handed it to the teller instead. He was so impressed that he gave me a brand new twenty-dollar bill.” The girl tries to imagine what she would do with twenty dollars. Probably buy a hamster.

•

As they head out to dinner in their silver Honda Accord, the woman’s husband suggests a restaurant he’s heard is good.

When they arrive, she says, “I’ve been here before.”

“Is it good?” he asks.

She laughs. “I don’t know. I haven’t been here since I was a kid.”

The woman scans everything around her as the hostess shows them to their table. From the cracking green leather booths, to the water cups, laminated menus, and the paper placemats with scalloped edges, it feels like a time capsule of “old school” restaurants that she remembers from childhood, long before the rise of fast casual dining and the sleek farm-to-table movement.

“Did you know this building used to be a bank?” she asks her husband. “The teller windows were over there. And the vault was behind that wall.”

“No way. How do you know that?”

“My grandparents banked here. Once, as a kid, my dad found a lost gold watch. The teller was so impressed he’d turned it in, that he gave him twenty dollars as a reward.”

“The same kid who used an axe to chop down the neighbor lady’s ornamental hedges?”

The woman smiles. “My grandma made him put the money in his piggy bank. But she was so proud of him, that on their way home she bought him an ice cream cone at Thrifty’s.”

"Damn, I really wish I could have met him," her husband shakes his head.

"I know. Me too," she says.

They sit in silence for a few moments.

Then the woman says, "Hey, there's a coyote hidden somewhere in those stained-glass windows. Do you see him?"

The Captain
Daniel Vidri

Damia Meglasson

Oblivion

The first to go are the little things. What you had for breakfast, whether you locked the door or not, the reason why you walked into a particular room, or the name of that park you loved as a kid, the one with the brightly colored pomegranate tree that stood out from the sickly yellow of the dead grass encircling it. It starts subtly, never making you wonder if something is wrong because it happens to everyone right?

Next to go are the faces of childhood acquaintances, what the correct finger positions are for playing the flute, what day of the week it is, where you put that damn hair tie, but panic is still far from your mind. It's all perfectly reasonable since it's been a while and after all, time flies when you're not paying attention.

When you start forgetting what you did the day before, paired with the uncertainty of when events took place, when you hesitate in your thoughts while attempting to think of a childhood friend's name, you finally feel the barest hints of anxiety seeping into your consciousness. But as quick as it appears, it's banished by the numerous excuses your mind comes up with to ease the dissonance.

The unease returns when you begin to question early memories. Did they actually happen or are they dreams you had? Was that hallucination episode just a nightmare? Did you really push that toddler off a slide? How the hell did you make up blue spaghetti that smelled like week old broccoli? The awe you felt, graduating preschool in that castle of a church had to have been real… right? Driving by the geographical sites of the memories only seems to heighten the uncertainty. What's remembered as a castle is a hovel, what event you believed to be fact isn't recalled by anyone else, the memories are now foggy at best and leave a sour taste in your mouth from a meal you don't remember eating.

You eventually feel like you're playing an endless game of hide and seek with your memories that you know existed, but the only thing you're left with is a ghost image where they used to reside and the panic and frustration that wells up inside you. You are unable to remember their contents anymore, just that you had them and now you don't. The name of the disease you've been afflicted with has long since been lost to you, any time it may have come back has left no trace behind. You are unsure if there are still those that care for you or if somehow the miraculously stocked fridge was your own doing.

Most days you contemplate if this state would follow you into the afterlife, if letting go would stop this malady in its tracks. Perhaps it would bring back all that you've lost, perhaps it would not but allow you to keep what you gain. There is no evidence in the house of a specific belief system, but you're not sure if you would remember the mythology anyway. With everything gone, hope of recovery, family and friends, the only fear left is that of the cycle resetting. Living again only to eventually forget with no chance of recovering. What is the point of knowledge gained if it is destined to eventually be lost? The most merciful fate then, would be instead to be cast into oblivion, never to return, never to hope, never to forget.

Up Close
Daniel Vidri

Mick Miles

Valley Isle Runaway

Beth and Gavin Watts are what some of the other renters have called a "power-couple", and I would almost agree if I didn't know so much about Gavin.

See, I just watch the grounds: I'm the on-site property manager, and it's a nice gig because I get a substantial discount on my rent. The downside is that I'm the one who has to deal with everyone's complaints, and I'm the guy who has to fix the broken things. I learned early on that if I invite a complaining tenant into my place for a glass of whiskey, the broken things go away, and the complaints turn into compliments: *you make a great Manhattan!*

Now Gavin Watts, this guy tends to have a lot of broken things, and a lifetime of complaints. If my apartment were a *real bar*, Gavin would be a regular. This guy LOVES to talk, and all the other renters, in turn, love to talk about him. Usually, I hate listening to renter gossip, but Beth and Gavin Watts stories are so entertaining! Gavin is a total asshole to his wife! Better yet are the beautiful and empowering ways of poetic justice in which Beth gets back at him. Yet despite all the verbal abuse and calculated retaliation, they're together every morning for routine exercise: daily workout partners.

Beth and Gavin's lives revolve around physical fitness. That's mostly true about Gavin, who works as a nutritionist and product developer for a start-up focused on producing all-natural protein shakes. Beth, on the other hand, works in early childhood development, and from what I've heard, has single handedly raised the overall literacy rate in her school's special needs program by 15%. And though Beth's job is infinitely more important, it's the lifestyle brought on by Gavin's job that shapes the way the Watts live their lives. He makes her run, swim and bike with him nearly every day. He records their times and the things they'd eaten to compile data and in turn, he's able to fine-tune his protein recipe. And from what I've heard listening to this guy, he's never happy with the results, and it's all the fault of his wife (who, "can't keep up"). That's the best part though, because I think she ran away from him—on foot!

There are a lot of different versions of the story, but this is what I've pieced together and filled in with imagination. Understand that the only way to tell the story is in the way I've heard it; that is, in Gavin's comically flawed perspective. He thinks he's the victim!

•

The alarm clock was blaring maddeningly in the bedroom and this was the second time. That meant it was 5:02. What the hell could Beth be dreaming so deeply about that she couldn't hear that loud, obnoxious music!? *Soooo damn lazy,* he thought. That's 18 full minutes of lost action. If it weren't for him, he was pretty sure Beth would sleep into the afternoon like a damn grade-schooler on summer break. *Ugghhh,* Gavin thought, *Beth would have turned out to be just like her parents if it weren't for me—fat and diabetic and gross!* It really pissed him off.

It repulsed him to think that you could spend so much of your time developing a routine with someone just to have them continually crap on your shared progress. He felt he needed to hold Beth's hand at every moment, lest the idiotic woman stray away and start pursuing *art* in her free time again. *That's love*, Gavin thought, and the sentiment made him feel good about himself, so he decided to let her go on sleeping. Maybe the blender would wake her up?

It didn't though, and that *really* got his goat.

"Beth! Behhhhhhhhh-th!" He yelled straight to her face as he hovered over her in bed. From up-close, he could see all of her flaws. He wished she'd apply makeup before going to bed.

She answered on the second yell.

"Good morning baby. How'd you sleep?" She said in a sweet tone of fake naivety.

"Perfectly adequate, thank you! And I didn't need half of the damn morning to do it!" He quipped sharply. "Did you *not* hear the alarm!? That's three times it's gone off now. Three times! Twenty-seven minutes; almost half an hour! You're killing our progress, Beth!"

"I'm sorry, I'm really tired. That swim yesterday *killed* me. What's in today's delicious and powerful smoothie?" She said, as if flattery could change the subject.

"Same as yesterday, only I added some bovine placenta extract and ground bullhorn compound," Gavin said, deciding to humor her. "But I drank yours, *Lazy-ass,* because you slept too long and proved to me that you really don't care about any of this... Now get up! C'mon! I don't want to waste any more time listening to your excuses. 'I'm so tired', oh, 'I swam so much' – yeah right! You were lagging yesterday, too; did you really think I'd buy that?"

Gavin turned to walk away and caught the *pretend-to-be-hurt* look on her face. He imagined she was pouting quietly to herself and lamenting that he wasn't going to hand-feed her like some infantile creature. Yes, she was probably so distraught to think that she'd have to make a shake for *herself* or grab a banana on the way out. He could hear it all in the sounds she let out: that pathetic *tssss* noise she made anytime she wanted to argue but knew she didn't have shit to say.

Beth, Beth, Beth: so predictable and easy to read, he thought as he looked around the room for his fit-bit watch.

"Babe, I can't find my fit-bit. See, this is why I can't stand when you clean, because you think you have to reorganize everything and then I can't find my things. I mean, are you just toying with me? Just trying to get a reaction? Playing hide and seek?" Gavin begged of her.

Yet again, instead of just responding in a civilized way (like an adult!), she buried her face in her pillow and started to scream. He wondered how many pillows she had ruined with her screaming little hissy fits. It's probably why she never slept well: all that negativity being constantly pushed and then trapped into the fabric caused her nightmares.

Finally, Gavin located the watch connected to its USB charging port and wondered why she would charge it when the battery wasn't anywhere close to being dead. He was sure it was for the same reason that she was now hauled up in the bathroom crying: to shorten life spans, both the battery of the watch and of he himself.

He wasn't going to let her ruin his good mood, he decided. Outside, he loaded the bikes into the Xterra and waited.

For several minutes, he drove in silence, deciding not to give into Beth's bitchy silent treatment. He was perfectly content just listening to the soothing, intelligent voices of two geneticists debating on NPR. The topic was nature vs. nurture.

"In a 2010 study by UC Berkley's psychology department, twins separated at birth and raised in dramatically different home environments displayed identical personality traits, to a startling

degree. This would argue for an inherent code for behavior, one we may be able to locate thanks to the Human Genome Project..." One geneticist went on.

Gavin realized that he had better turn down the volume and set the record straight before these NPR bozos brainwashed his Beth.

"See, Beth, this is where I disagree with what these guys are saying. If you gather 20 people who are all characteristically kind, well-raised individuals—like me, or, I guess, like you—and you put them into a room with jail cells, and you assign five of those people to be the guards, no matter how sweet and fair they may be based on some *genetic code*, those five people will turn into nasty, power monger drill sergeants. That was proven with that Alcatraz Experiment. So, you can't go saying nature plays no role whatsoever in shaping our behavior." Gavin informed proudly. He loved it when he could prove to Beth that her man was smarter than any dummy with a PhD.

Then, of course, Beth—the perennial voice of fact-checkers everywhere—spoke up to undermine his concise brilliance.

"Yeah, well that is *not* the point he's making, and if you had just listened to what the other doctor was going to say, you'd see that they're having a conversation that lends credence to both schools of thought. Your argument is about something completely different: the nature of power." She said in a snotty, know-it-all tone of voice.

"You're still mad at me, huh?" Gavin prodded. He knew that's what this was all about, this little act of disagreement.

Beth remained silent, like he *knew* she would, because he had seen right through her silly little ruse. *She might be able to fool the half-wits at school with that type of charade,* he thought, *but not me, sweetheart!*

"It's like I'm always saying," Gavin began to quote himself, in an effort to get back to the radio discussion, "'people can't be defined by any one action, because we're all collective surprise bags of thousands of personalities'. If someone pisses you off in a way you thought they weren't capable of, that's because a different *personality* committed that wrongdoing. We switch it up almost *entirely* based on our *environment.* Nature is everything. Nurture is, A: not a big factor in development, and B: not even that necessary."

Beth was hardly paying attention, it seemed, because her response to this very well-phrased, educated counter argument was to put Gavin down and try to make it a firefight.

"Ooh, what was it?" she mocked, "a '*collective surprise bag of thousands of personalities'?* Well then why are you always such an asshole, Gavin? I don't see any of the other thousands of personalities. And I'm not *surprised.*"

He wanted so badly to squash her with a seething verbal assault but thought better of it. He knew he was too nice, too *smart* to fall into her trap. He decided instead to turn it around on her so she could see how mean she could be.

"Geez, Beth, is name calling really necessary? Is that what you teach the children? I'm not trying to say anybody is wrong here, I'm just giving you my take. Yet here you are, finding a way to put me down—me—the guy who loves you, who married you, who keeps you focused on our goals…"

"I know," she said, "I'm sorry. You're right. That was uncalled for, and definitely not what I teach my students. I guess you're right and I am just upset about earlier. You didn't have to wake me up in such a rude way and I can't believe you drank my smoothie—"

"Beth! It's a shake! A protein *shake*! Christ, grab a banana on your way out next time! Or make an oatmeal, or…"

He parked the car by Kama'ole Beach Park, where they got out and stretched on the grass just as the sun settled its gaze across the calm morning ocean. Gavin expressed his displeasure at how late they were starting.

"…And god, Beth, please, *please*, no stopping this time. Please, just try to keep up a decent pace and don't break from it. I need you to actually *run* the whole time. If you're stopping and going, stopping and going all the time, I have no inkling how my protein blend performs in female athletes." As soon as he said it, he remembered that she hadn't woken up in time for her shake, nor had she been motivated enough to feed herself. He didn't feel bad, though, because he knew how bioaccumulation worked and that her body was still teeming with proteins from days before.

Much to her credit, Beth did not protest. When she wanted to be, Beth was a woman of tough mental fortitude—it was one of the reasons he had married her—and on this morning in particular, she seemed to be trying to prove just that. Though he started uncharacteristically fast, she kept up. Gavin never listened to music while running because he didn't want the pace of the song to influence the pace of his stride, but at that moment, the song in his mind was *Sisters Are Doing it for Themselves,* by the Eurythmics:

Now there was a time when they used to say
That behind every – great man.
There had to be a – great woman.
But in these times of change you know
That it's no longer true.
So we're comin' out of the kitchen
'Cause there's somethin' we forgot to say to you (we say)
Sisters are doin' it for themselves.
Standin' on their own two feet.

Indeed, there she was, standing on her own two feet and running with purpose. It made Gavin so proud that he was beginning to forgive her for delaying their routine. Twenty-five minutes later and Beth was still right there with him (if not a tad bit behind) and for his part, Gavin was feeling strong like a gold medal champion. He even broke out into an all-or-nothing sprint when they approached the hill at Kilohana Drive. The gentle morning rays felt great on his shoulders and the smell of blooming plumerias made him want to own the entire neighborhood. He was feeling powerful, but also pleasant.

Yet by the crest of the hill, Beth started to show her true colors again. Defeating the great hill had aroused and energized him, and by contrast, Beth was trudging along laboriously, as if the hill had defeated *her.* He looked back to see the pain written all over her face, and it made him scoff in disapproval.

He wasn't going to slow his pace for her, not when he was feeling this driven and supreme. The sun was beating down on him already, but it was too late for the Sun God. Gavin had started too early, had already begun to claim the cracked streets for himself. Soon he would be diving into the ocean where he would cut through the water like a speedboat back to the spot where he had parked his Xterra. At that point, it would be only a matter of time. And sure as shit, Beth had *wasted* a lot of that time, and it would be extremely hot out when he would finally get to ride his bike. *Oh well. Bring it.* He couldn't wait for the final showdown on the Lahaina Pali Trail: a man and his bike against a titan. It was to Gavin a very blood-pumping daydream, and he smiled, knowing he'd outwork the sun.

But then, Beth threw up.

She threw up vehemently, painting an entire block of sidewalk as red-orange as a hibiscus with a single blast. He stopped to see her body tremor from her core and on through her shoulders and face. Then out came another, smaller blast of puke. With her back arched and her hands placed on her knees, she hyperventilated for recovery.

"My *god*!" he said, "are you *kidding* me!?" He ran back to her, further down the hill.

He watched as the dry heaving began. She sounded like some kind of dragon: a pathetic, dying dragon. He unzipped his fanny pack and retrieved a small water bottle, which he passed to her. She snatched it from his hands with surprising zest.

"That's it, Beth," he said, "let out all of the weakness. Is that even possible?"

She chugged some water and glared at him. He had seen that glazed look before; he realized now that this was a hangover.

"Guess you drank a little more than *one* glass of wine with your little teaching buddy last night, huh? Got a little wasted, tried to hide it? It's okay, though, Beth, because look at that: the truth is literally written all over the sidewalk!"

She just continued to look up at him, her strands of licorice-red hair stuck to her sweaty forehead, spit dribbling from the corner of her mouth.

"I didn't have any breakfast!" she blurted, as if in defense.

"And whose fault is that?" said Gavin. "You slept in, and you chose to leave without eating anything."

She shook her head in what looked like disgust and it triggered him.

"Well I don't know what that look was, but I don't even care. And I don't care that today's routine has been ruined—by you—I don't care, Beth. I feel great. I really think *this* was the perfect blend today. I'll make the same shake tomorrow, and you'll see. We'll get this right, and then you'll see. I've found the *perfect* protein blend." Gavin said with authority.

She continued shaking her head and clenching her teeth.

"Look," he said, deciding to go with a calmer tone, "babe, I'm sorry. I'm sorry you don't feel good, and we don't even have to keep running. We don't have to keep running, we don't have to get in the water or ride our bikes, because I'm telling you, I've created a perfect shake. This mixture, I just know, I can market it any number of ways and it wouldn't even matter; I feel like an animal because of this shake from this morning. Look, tomorrow, we'll run it back. You'll wake up the *first* time the alarm goes off. You won't get wasted tonight. We'll both have a nice breakfast, and you'll try the shake I make, and you'll feel like I do now. You'll feel great."

Then, out of nowhere and much to his surprise, she stood upright. She wiped her mouth with her forearm, cracked her neck joints on both sides, and grabbed a handful of his spandex shirt.

"I feel great *now!"* Beth yelled demonically at him.

Gavin whipped his head back in trepidation. Beth gulped down the rest of the water and crushed the plastic bottle in her hand. She gasped for air and looked him in the eyes with a piercing, almost hostile stare.

"Alright," he said dismissively, "let's start walking then…" He threw his hands in the air in frustrated disbelief.

"You can do whatever you want, *Gavin,"* Beth said venomously, "I don't care, *Gavin*, because I feel great!" And with that, she burst out into a sprint.

"What the hell are you doing!?" Gavin yelled after her. "Beth! You're going the wrong way!" *What is she thinking?* He wondered curiously. He decided just to watch her, to see how far she'd get. *No way she makes it past the bend.* Yet not only did she make it, she even started to pick up speed. He felt confused but challenged. *So, it's a race she wants?* He thought, and he started to chase after her.

•

"I mean, how is it even possible to keep up a pace like that? With nothing in your system? Hung-over, with god only knows what the hell else in her system. My wife…" Gavin told me one day, long after she had disappeared. "…My wife displayed very strange behavior that day, *very strange!* I don't know what kinds of drugs she might have taken the night before with her *slut* friend Katie!"

I listened to him as I swirled the Speyside single malt around in my glass. I didn't know what to say other than to ask if she was safe, or if he tried to contact her family. At that, he just laughed, said yes, laughed some more, and then assured me (me? himself?) that she'd be back.

All accounts of the story—from the other renters who claim to have spotted Beth running, to Gavin himself—say that he chased her well past the beach park where they had parked their car and all through the length of Kihei. Beth: always just a dashing figure on Gavin's horizon, forever moving forward until she got far, far away. He tells me he gave up, not out of fatigue ("It's like I said, I felt like an animal that day" he'd say), but out of a lack of care, just around the animal shelter on the Mokulele Highway.

Other sources tell me they both ran much further than that, being spotted on the Hana Highway heading into Paia; Beth always just a dashing figure on Gavin's horizon, forever moving forward, from late morning on through the day and into the night. I'd like to think that she ran all the way to the Hana Airport, had her father transfer her some money, and hopped on a Cessna and flew to Honolulu International, where she could depart to any far away city in the world. Hopefully she did just that, and got far, far away from Gavin. Because *forget* guys like that—they talk too damn much.

Gray Bird
ShuJen Walker

Duncan Mullis

Calluses

I have calluses just below my fingers

They're raised and numb, worn, signs of wear and tear. When I touch them, they are rough. They are a darker color than the rest of my hands. They offer grip to the things I want to grab. They are badges of achievement that keep building as I work. They are awards given to me after a long day of exercise. They are sweat and sterilizer spray and weights and mirror pictures of my biceps. After I use them, they hurt.

They also represent fear. They are the marks of me clawing my way away from my body. Where it stands just behind door frames, looking out. I see it trapped in the mirror, tapping the glass, in car windows and my front-facing camera. It looks at me, and I look back. I turn away.

At twelve years old I didn't have calluses. My hands were new. No veins showed below the skin. My fingers were small and smooth, perfect for playing video games and reading books. Perfect for twanging small notes on a ¾ sized guitar. Perfect for eating hummus and pita chips in front of the T.V. They were perfect for carrying a skateboard to the smooth asphalt of my apartment complex. Perfect for eating Nutella sandwiches in front of the T.V. Perfect for holding wooden swords. Perfect for making breakfast for my mother, whose bed was in the living room, and her boyfriend, who slept there. Perfect for grabbing the fat around my stomach.

My hands were small and pudgy, like Cee Lo Greens, and Jack Black's. They had no calluses.

My hair was long. It reached my shoulders, got in my eyes. I cut it myself, I watched the hair go into the trash, and down the toilet. It smelled funny, old and musty. The shampoo got caught in the sides of my hair. It got matted, hard to brush out. Dad said It looked better short, but he lived in a different house. Mom said she liked it better long anyway. It looked like her boyfriend, who slept there sometimes.

His hair was long and dark, and he was blind in one eye. He had a scar that ran across his stomach, from a knife fight he had been in, and a soul patch. When he came home early, he brought

Hawaiian pizza home. When he came home late, he was loud. He woke us up sometimes, to shout at us. He said things like "Look at that fat tummy!" and "You're so fucking lazy".

Mom said I wasn't fat, Mom said I was just dense. I had always been built like that, she said, as had my whole family. That I should eat the Nutella sandwiches, and the hummus and pita bread. I am a growing boy. I need the calories.

I wore fleeces and shirts that said "Get a Life" with the green Mario mushroom on them. I liked to play bass for the band. I listened to the White Stripes. Ball and Biscuit was my favorite song.

I hated the pool and the beach, where I thought people looked at me. I didn't want to look at me.

I liked dragons and myths and Lord of the Rings. I liked how Legolas could surf down the staircase at Helms Deep on an orc shield, shooting arrows on the way down. I liked to watch Aragorn charge headlong into battle, screaming. I wanted to do that, to be them.

Except, I couldn't. I couldn't run without losing my breath or bend down to touch my toes. I couldn't lift the sword that Aragorn used, or pull back the bowstring of Legolas. The fat kid didn't get the kiss at the end, he didn't get to charge into battle or go to the Undying Lands. the fat kid has one purpose: to take up space.

I hated showering, I hated looking in the mirror. I hated looking at pictures of myself, I hated the way other people looked at me. I hated the way my mother's boyfriend, who stays at our house sometimes, looked at me. Like I was in the way. Like I took up too much space.

I liked Nutella, and Hawaiian pizza. I liked macaroni and cheese, with peas and hot dogs in them, and Top Ramen, and chips and hummus. I ate them in front of the T.V, and I turned it up really loud. It helped drown out everything else.

They have feasts in Lord of the Rings. Merry and Pippin love their second breakfast. They have it all the time in the shire. And the hobbits are skinny. Frodo was thin, and he carried the ring, and he had a Second Breakfast. I want a second breakfast. Why can't I have a second breakfast?

Those days were almost a decade ago.

My body still haunts me. I can see a twelve-year-old boy hiding behind door frames, peeking into my room. I can see him when I look in the mirror, tapping on the glass. I can feel his pudgy hands, perfect for grabbing every ounce of fat still attached to my body. I can smell him when I miss a shower or forget to brush my teeth. I can taste him when I eat Top Ramen, and Macaroni and Cheese with peas and hot dogs. When I eat Hawaiian pizza, more than one slice.

I see him as I try to fall asleep. I dream of the treadmill, of hard things, weights, sanitizer and exercise. I dream of sweat and muscles and veins. I dream of flat stomachs and glistening abs and taking my shirt off in public. In my dream, the gym is empty, save for two people. Me, who exercises, and Him, who watches, with a frown on his face. I run faster.

I can now lift the sword and pull the bowstring. I can charge into the din of battle and surf down a staircase and shoot people with arrows, or at least I can try.

My mother lives in a different state.

Her boyfriend, who stayed over sometimes, has left.

And I now have calluses, just below my fingers,
to show how far I've crawled away from them.

The Graveyard Poet

"And this is where I lock him away."

I looked at the book Josie was holding. A medium sized grey notebook, with leather overlapped corners. It had an old tattered band-aid where the title should be and scrawled upon it in angular letters read *The Daft Graveyard Poet,* she was cradling it like a child.

"What does that mean?" I asked, gesturing to the title.

She brushed her hair out of the way and laughed a small laugh.

"It wasn't originally going to be named that. When I put the band-aid on I was going to write my name," she pursed her lips and stared at the bedsheets. "But then I thought about the contents of the book itself. And realized that It was a stupid-dead-girl-songbook, and I was the Graveyard Poet."

I cocked my head.

"I wrote poems from the grave, because I knew no one else would read them, so it was as if the writing itself was dead.... If that makes sense?"

I smiled "Totally, dude. The Daft Graveyard Poet."

"Has a nice ring to it, doesn't it?"

"I mean, you certainly are daft." I said with a grin; she laughed, slugged me on the arm. We scooted closer. And she opened the book.

•

Josie has auburn hair, the color of a redwood tree.

Josie's auburn hair is dyed to the color of midnight.

This, accompanied by her blue eyes, reminds of a bright night on a shifting sea.

All her clothes are modified. She has not one item in her wardrobe that is in the same state as it was when she got it. They all bear the marks of her individuality, adorned with either holes, tears, or sharpie scrawls, sometimes all three.

Her room is littered with stories from adventures she's gone on. Every bauble a sentence, that makes a paragraph. The ink her story is written in. A couple baubles were mine.

Anyone looking at her would see a cult classic high-school movie punk girl archetype. The way she acts, the I-don't-care attitude. She puts off schoolwork to play guitar in the halls for an audience. *She's the coolest kid on the block.*

But that's not her. That's her cellmate, Jimmy.

•

She flipped through the book to show me it's contents. Sketches of people, the lines hard and angular, littered them. Poems, askew from the set lines, read rhymes, surrounded by sketched emblems known only to her. One I saw over and over, as we flipped through her thoughts.

"What is that one?" I asked, pointing to a little symbol. An upside-down cross with a heart laid upon it. Knowing her, it had a meaning. She never did anything without a meaning.

"That's Saint Jimmy's cross." She didn't take her eyes from the pages.

"Josie, do I look like I know who Saint Jimmy is?"

"No," she conceded. "But you don't look like you know much of anything else, either."

"Touché."

She smirked. "It's a Green Day thing. Saint Jimmy is the Jesus of Suburbia's alter ego. The Patron Saint of Chaos and the Underground, he was born with a pistol in his right hand and a syringe in his left."

"You looked that up just now."

She shook her head and flashed a smile, quickly faded. "It's hard to explain, there are a lot of moving parts."

She stared into the distance, lost in thought.

"The only way I could describe him is as my cellmate."

I cocked a brow but remained silent.

"There's a room in my head. It has cement walls, no doors, and no windows. There are two recliner chairs facing an old CRT T.V." She glanced at me. I nodded to continue. "One is for me, and the other is for Jimmy. The T.V. Shows what I see out of my eyes. And Jimmy has the remote. Does that sound stupid?"

I sat and thought about this. "Not at all."

She nodded. "Jimmy is a part of me. He says things that I don't want to hear. Things like 'you look stupid, you're too fat, no one will ever love you."

I flared up at this. "He sounds like a total asshole. You should tell him to fuck off."

She shook her head. "He is just trying to protect me. He's not a bad guy, just misguided… You have to have sympathy for him."

I sat there for a while, processing. This entire concept was a lot to take in.

"You astound me sometimes."

"All the time," she corrected.

I rolled my eyes. "All the time." Silence.

"Wanna put on the movie now?" I managed.

"Yeah man." she said with a smirk, and we exited her room to watch a cult classic and drink vodka shots chased down with pickle juice, as was tradition.

But I wasn't paying attention to *Detroit Rock City*, or how dizzy I was feeling. All I could think about was Jimmy. A voice in your head, criticizing you. Making you feel like shit. His harsh words force you into bed for months, paralyzed by the hands he uses to hold you down. It sounded hauntingly familiar.

After Josie had picked up the remnants of our little party and had gone to bed, I laid upon the couch and stared up to the ceiling. I thought about my life, and the role my very own Saint Jimmy had played in it.

I thought about 2014, when dangling from a belt seemed like the best way to silence the whispering in my ears.

I thought about how in that dark time, I rarely said those things to myself in the first person. When my thoughts had run away from me, *I* never thought "I am Worthless."

It was always framed in Second Person. "*You are worthless. You are fat. You are ugly. No one will ever love you; you should kill yourself. Now.*" And I just happened to agree. My Jimmy spoke *to* me, and just happened to be very persuasive in his arguments. Hot breath on my neck.

I thought about how his silhouette was in the corner that day. His echo. Watching me dangle and thrash. He felt disappointed.

But there were two parts to what Josie had said. One Part is that He exists, and he exists in everyone. He is the inner voice telling you to shut the fuck up or sit the fuck down. *You are fucking stupid, die, you fat piece of shit. Die.* Everyone has that, everyone's Jimmy is different, everyone manages them in a different way.

But the second part that Josie revealed was his True Nature.

Jimmy is a misguided soul, not an antagonist. He is the voice in the dark of the mind, hurt, huddled in a corner, fighting all he can to stay alive. I can't fight him. He is not something that should be defeated. He was a part of me, as much as my haircut or my music tastes, and I don't hate those for just existing.

My philosophy at the time was that there is never a problem you can't face head on. Punch, kick, claw, scratch. Fight dirty. Whatever it takes to get to the top. All else is Cowardice.

This new taste of love for my enemy was something I had not heard of before. So, I decided to give it a shot.

The next couple years I reformed. I would listen to Jimmy whenever he appeared. I would heed the whispers in my ear and meet them with a warm embrace. I would see a vague shape flit behind the counter as I placed my fast food order, hear the harsh voice in my ear: *Of course you get fast food, what else would you expect from a fat fuck such as yourself*

And I would say "Jimmy, I love you." And that would be that. He would sit there, stunned. What can he use against me?

Now I can feel his guiding hand. His breath on my neck is not a sign of foreboding, but comfort. I know what he's there for.

Jimmy is the morals in the mind. *The scales that tip and balance. The Gavel and the Rope.* He is the drive to self-improvement. Freud calls him the Superego, He goes by many names, and he goes by one. *Jimmy. Jimmy. Jimmy.*

He is the one reforging my relationship with my parents.

You shouldn't have said that. You need to apologize. Tell them you love them.

He is the one who siphons the words from my tongue, the iron to forge my stories.

That doesn't sound right. I would have the main character spare the antagonist.

He is the one sitting on the bench when I hand a beggar my change. I look into his gently glowing eyes. A silhouette of light.

A nod assents.

A smile.

•

I now live with my cellmate. I understand what he is and what he is meant to do. We share the remote.

Thank you, Daft Graveyard Poet. Stupid Dead-Girl. Jesus of Suburbia. Josie my friend, you showed me the way.

And thank you Saint Jimmy. You have earned your title. What you did was indispensable.

You kept me there.

Jessica Nelson

Adventures of Terrence Pepperidge

The smell of the room he resided in was as putrid as a carnival Port-a-Potty; wait that's exactly where he was. Terrence Pepperidge was not the strongest or the softest and he was only a single ply, but he was a reliable roll of toilet paper and he sadly had very few sheets of life left to give.

Most rolls have no goals other than to make it into the great blue bowl, however, Terrence dreamed of seeing the sights. From the beginning of his career, that morning, he'd been staring at a travel magazine that had been precariously thrown on the floor and was fascinated by the collage of monuments strewn across the cover.

A woman entered and sat down next to Terrence; he politely averted his eyes to the magazine as she went about her business. After a while, the lady proceeded to pull Terrence all the way down to the cardboard, he felt so exposed, he was terrified and knew this was the end of his mission and in turn the end of his life. But wait! When the woman finished defiling him, his tail got stuck on the woman's skirt, the parchment gods had bestowed upon him a glorious privilege and, as his benevolent transporter stepped out of the Port-a-Potty, he was bathed in multicolored lights and the smell of buttered popcorn. The glimpses he'd had of the outside world didn't nearly do it justice.

A few children giggled and pointed at Terrence whispering, "Look that woman has TP stuck in her skirt." Terrence wondered how the kids knew his initials, but he was too excited and just waved at them as his host walked past. Tons of people were lined up in front of the rides. Terrence saw the "Eiffel Tower", a ride that forced people up into the air and dropped them down just above the ground, he was happy when his transporter passed that ride, it was far too scary. There was a fun house called "The Sphinx", and a ride with little boats that took you through the Nile river… it was much smaller than Terrence expected. Nonetheless, Terrence was wildly impressed by it all.

The most impressive ride was the "Ferris Wheel", cages carried people to the very top of a giant wheel and slowly brought them back down. Terrence was ecstatic when his host joined another human at the front of the line. All three got on the ride and were floating above the ground in no time. As they reached the top of the wheel Terrence could see the whole world right in front of him it was marvelous, he saw everything he'd been yearning to see.

The top of the ride was windy and as they sat there, a large gust tore Terrence out of the top of the woman's skirt and sent him soaring through the sky, past the "Eiffel Tower," past the Nile river, past "The Sphinx," and down to the ground where he landed in a small puddle of water. He knew this was the end of his life, but he wasn't sad or scared, he was happy. He'd done more than any roll could have dreamed of; he'd seen the world. As he dissolved into the water, he silently thanked the woman.

E.R. O'Connor

Plastic Playground

"That was, *Painkillers* by Rainbow Kitten Surprise and your listenin' to '*Live* From Your Grave' on KMS 96.6 Radio." Angel's nails skip along with the soundboard switches, and I follow behind, "If you're just tunin' in, I'm your host 'Spookie' Stern."

"And I'm Angel Bell."

"Comin' up, *Chemical Sweat* by Elliot Root. So, sit back, and let the night take you."

She shakes off her headphones as the song's tempo titters out to our listeners, looking past me to a twitching clock about to slap five, "You know, we're gonna have to answer some of those *psycho killer* calls soon — and they're creepier after three. God, I hate those freaks."

Not entirely sliding off my pair but freeing my left ear from its musky tomb enough to hear her whispered church voice, I roll my eyes, already annoyed, "I'll take them."

"What?"

"I'll take the calls."

"Don't fuck with me, Stevie." I raise my eyebrows at her last turn of phrase, the nonchalant use of my real name, to show I'm serious. Angel presses her palms together in worship, "Bless you," she stands, "You're Mother fuckin' Teresa! You've got wings, baby!"

The surprise of her sermon calls my suppressed laugh out of the pitiful cave it's been hiding in since I left Tom, but before I can respond, Angel and her sable skin have floated out the portal to the real world. In the empty, I miss her talons; how they can teleport us from one track to another. She'd painted them ruby red in the last hour, studying my sulk as they dried.

When I adjust the tempo, my own digits are out of place — fish fingers out of water.

"I'm absolutely in love with their album, so don't be surprised if you hear a lot more of Elliot Root in the comin' weeks." Angel hasn't yet made her way back into the studio, I shouldn't take the call, not without her in the seat beside me, but something about the pulsar beaming atop our phone beckons my fishtail finger to push into it. To break protocol. “Before we dive back into your favorite tunes, let’s hear from some of our listers, shall we?”

The words, which have always been empty, abruptly shift. They feel as if I’m standing in a crowded room, my back being brushed by strangers’ hands as they pass searching for dance partners, “You’re on with Spookie, what’s your name caller?”

There’s someone on the other side, breathing, sacrificing a silent second to radio waves.

Finally, he gulps, “Theo,” and I know he’s lying. I can hear it in the sound his tongue makes as it hits his teeth. His human noise fascinates me. I know it.

I’m entranced by the gulp, by the hesitant breath waiting behind it, and the vibration drops me from my spinning seat to a stationary sofa. I slide out of a desolate booth and into a fluid house party, one pumping music through its veins and thrusting it into me. In my bones, the gulp is calculated, measured as my thighs press against frosted denim and my posture leans too far over his — I feel his swallow also, as it runs through his toes nervously. Not only does the seat cress my spine, prop me high enough to allow his nose to nuzzle into my neck, but it also makes me a passenger — a fresh pair of silver eyes to long in a seat beside the driver. A hand reaches out to meet mine from behind a steering wheel, but back then he didn’t say ‘Theo.’

No, before I kiss him across the console, he chokes out, “Thomas.”

I can’t bring myself to call him by any other name, not since I’d said it twice within my vows, it’s the only promise I can still keep to him. “How ya doin’ tonight?” I cough the same question as always; my thoughts echoing out across Louisiana, a lump rising in my throat, and a terror crawling behind my ears.

He hesitates, as if in shock that it’s my voice that comes across the line, not Angel’s. The caller clears his throat, forcing back down the first sentence he’s come up with and settling for, “I’ve been better, Stevie.”

“What’s on your mind?” I have to stop myself before slurring his name in a beautiful drunk state. As much as a portion of my being is compelled to hang up, another piece, one much smaller at the center of my heart is desperate to hear his speech for another second.

Feet move, he paces, “My wife left me, says she wants a divorce,” The speaker rattles with his skull, “To be honest, your show is the only thing getting me through it, hearing you talk every night is comforting. I just — I don't know what happened."

"I hear ya," Talking is trying, "I'm goin' through something like that myself."

There's another long pause on his part, he's thinking, but then comes back to life.

"How does it hurt?" First, his question puzzles me, I hear it in another voice, the one he offers to patients, but never me. It's only after another click of his tongue hits the mic that I feel an ache in my chest. It'd been there before I picked up, lurking four paces behind as I packed the car. It was on *that* evening that I'd discovered my pain was serrated, it had sawed my will to walk away in half from sheer fear. For a second, *then*, I'd considered turning back, but his black curls and watering eyes would have brought me to my knees. I would have sung hymns instead of sliding through the wooden cracks in our marriage. So, I never saw him. I never saw the expression he held as I departed.

There's an echo I recognize, I know it because I've made it myself. He's standing in the garage, staring the titanium door down, and waiting — waiting for my return. "It feels like I'm standin' at a sick bed, watchin' a version of myself wither away," I stop, listening to his breath rise, "The version I wish I were."

"Then why'd you leave him?"

"I used to dream he'd talk to me," I say quietly, as if bashful of the excuse, "That'd he'd tell me about the days I sleep through, but I'm always on the other side of the door." My hand presses to glass that doesn't exist, hopeful his own is extending as well.

Something shuts, a cabinet, "What if he forgot how?" Cups clink hitting granite, "Forgot how to talk to you, I mean." The caller goes on, "What if he's listening instead?"

The question is evocative, I can't tell what he's implying, but it still drags a nail up my spine, making my hair fall forward as I sigh against it. I know he's not there, not standing behind me as he speaks, but I feel him. I feel his arms drape over my shoulders like a scarf, I feel his lips press into my skull before his chin finds a spot atop my head, I feel his warmth against each knotted bone in my back. Crickets chirp from his side, and grass crunches under mud stained sneakers. I close my eyes imagining the creaky porch swing he breezes by, the overgrown front yard he's stepping through, and flowers being covered in a light layer of morning dew that his fingers tap; trying to decipher what he means, only to hear him sigh again, “I’m listening, Stevie. Just like you said, I’m listening.”

I’m quiet too, unable to see past my own thoughts, but then it comes back to me.

Remembering a jolted icicle stabbing the bottom of my foot as it slipped from the comforter to concrete, I gasp. The rug had wrinkled, moved out of the vicinity it was meant to linger within, leaving the floor frozen when the heater blew out. I dropped to my knees, searching for a slip of thrown lace, anything to cover my flesh before returning to the night, finding it after I swept my hand beneath the bed, and into the void of blackness that rested there. Silent I drew back, fearful that some lonely lurking creature would pull me under if I weren’t quick enough.

Tom stirred, he’d heard me catch my breath and fall off my supporting ankles in an attempt to escape a loathsome demon. He didn’t know me well enough to understand the horror I interpreted from the oil-soaked space. Hell, he didn’t know me well enough to remember the color of my eyes since the moon adjusted their tint; we’d only just met. However, Tom did know that I was the type of girl to follow home a man she’d known all of twenty minutes, he knew that I gurgled beer in the back of my throat and that I laughed anytime someone touched the backside of my tights — that I turned pink when he did. That was his favorite part of me, he’d later claim.

Knotted hair lifted from a pillow as he propped himself up, “What are you doing?”

The question was muddled by his tried vocal cords, and yet it’s still the same voice I can hear across the line now. To it, I smirked and pulled on the garment I’d discovered amongst dust bunnies, “I have to get to work,” I muttered, turning my attention to finding the pair of shorts I’d had on upon arrival, “I’m gonna be late.” I’d had a shirt too, but it was long gone.

“It’s nearly midnight.” Tom groaned again, sitting up and rubbing his eyes with the heel of his palm while he watched me spring about the loft. Beaming as I held up bottoms in triumph.

He looked worried, hurt as if I was leaving him without real cause, “I know,” I said making my way back to edge of the mattress on which he rested, “I know it sounds crazy, but trust me, I wouldn’t go if I didn’t have to.”

“Then don’t.” He smiled suddenly, looping his finger through the hem of the fabric against my hip, tethering me to him effectively. An electric laugh erupted from my lips, sounding juvenile, as if I were ten years younger chasing the boy I liked around a plastic playground.

"Temptin'," I shook my head, and it was, only the impending doom of Angel's wrath was a far stronger sensation, "But I really gotta go."

As he counted the freckles beneath my bra strap I slid out of grasp, trying to detangle my hair with my fingers as he reasoned aloud, "Stevie, wait, I don't even have your phone number," The line is strained by fear again, as if I was about to disappear forever, "How will I find you?"

I took a step closer, not enough for him to latch on as I was sure he hoped to, but near enough to the bedside table to turn on and re-tune his clock radio, "Listen." I said swiping a shirt of his from the floor and skipping towards the door — barefoot. Tom shook his head, I could hear him same as I do tonight, and unlike the last time I'd left him behind, I looked back. I squeezed my eyes shut and took a picture of him, of his folded knees and a crooked grin.

That polaroid still glowing in my head consumes me, and I begin to tear up, my elbows bent against the soundboard and my hands holding me up to the best of their ability. The water doesn't come from depression; it emerges from fury — pure delightful anger towards myself.

He'd called in the midst of *that* night's show, and I'd forgotten his name for nearly a full second — too distracted by Angel's catcalling and slut shaming to say it correctly. Something like, "Theo," slipped from my lips and he laughed. He forgave me, correcting the lie with a sly smirk slid across his cheeks, too pleased I'd answered to be upset. I'd heard that as well.

Eventually, I answer the comment he'd had before, that he'd been listening, "Really?"

It's that sly smirk, I can hear it in the sound his tongue makes as it hits his teeth, just off balance from the gulp, "Yes." I hear his human noise, his chin lifting to the morning sky, from there he asks something else, "Do you think, if *your* husband were listening, you'd go home?"

I laugh like I'm fifteen years younger, chasing the boy I like around a plastic playground. Abandoned by Angel, I feel silk and lace in different layers, heavy on my heart, trailing behind me, and from within my desolate booth I vow, “I do.” He sighs, pleased too, knowing I’ll stand by the porch swing again soon.

The line doesn’t die when it clicks out, it’s merely silent in joy.

The radio waves, the Gods, have accepted his tribute.

Like Angel, who has wings same as I, I fly to my feet and throw my headphones to the wind, offering them to caution; only stopping before I exit the studio to say, “You’re listenin’ to ‘*Live* From Your Grave’ on KMS 96.6 Radio. If you’re just tunin’ in, I’m your host ‘Spookie’ Stern. Comin’ up, *Heart Attack* by Wild Rivers. So, sit back, and let the night take you.”

Dee Richards

When I Was a Girl

Bright blobs of indeterminate construct; I can't move my body. Flashes of faces, full of delight, descend upon me. Their puckered lips kiss my cheeks, my forehead, my drooling mouth. My best friend's unblinking eyes keep watch over me between matted, white faux fur. His unyielding smile holds my attention; Snoopy, you are my only friend. I crave their arms to wrap me in warmth, so I cry. They give me a pacifier and another kiss.

Morning sun reflects on soft, blond hair, pulled tight into pigtails and emphasized by bright, pink ribbons. My small, pink and white dress hangs above white patent-leather shoes. I have a matching purse! I'm so grown up. My mom loves to show off her pretty, little dolly.

The sun shines brightest after school, casting shadows through the leaves. That boy from up the street just hit me. "He must like you," says my mom. Now he's all sparkly when I see him. The mirror tells me I need to look better, so he knows I like him, too. My stringy, dirty-blond hair hangs to my shoulders, I am wearing my favorite "Taz" shirt. My scuffed tennis shoes aren't Nikes, and my jeans aren't Levi's. Did I even brush my hair today? I ask my mom if I can borrow her lipstick, and she laughs as we put it on. We paint my nails, also, pink glitter. I have a skirt around here somewhere, don't I?

Flickering fluorescent casts a lifeless glow upon rows of lockers that I'm sure no one's ever used. Other girls have D-Cups! Why are mine only a B?! No wonder no one's asked me to the dance. A blue, velvet dress hangs in my closet, waiting. Should I eat breakfast today? Nah, I'll just have a Surge later. I walk with my eyes downcast, but Marcus stops me: "Hey, you know my boy Chris likes you?" He laughs, glancing down the hall. I see Chris chuckling with a few others. "Okay," I say, then keep on walking. I wonder what it would be like to kiss Chris.

A single desk lamp illuminates my green, polyester gown. How can I be graduating from high school next week and not even have had a boyfriend? I notice my jeans, my yellow Beastie Boys shirt; I think I look cool. At school, my friends talk about their first time, but I don't even know if I want to. "You're going to be a virgin forever," says my best friend, Kerry. "Yeah, just find a guy and do it!" Dana presses. "It's not that difficult," laughs Amber. My brother's friend says he's into me – maybe I can try with him. I choose my best flannel nightgown for when he comes over, and we head for my room. Beneath a dollar-store blacklight, he seems to be enjoying himself. I really can't do anything except stare at my Tigger silk-screen wall scroll. This isn't as great as they said.

Pounding darkness. 3... 4... 5... Am I... Am I already on my fifth drink?! My laughter has a mind of its own now. Do I remember that guy's name that just kissed me? My mind swims around the room. "It's getting hot in here – so take off all your clothes." Not my kind of music, but it's sorta fun. I fall into a leather loveseat; I just need to relax for a minute. Isn't that the guy I kissed? "Hey, I brought us some shots!" He says, and hands me one. "I think I gotta take it easy for a sec," I say. "Let's go upstairs and relax!" He smiles. I almost trip. "Don't be a lightweight!" He downs his shot. I'm really tired. He's kissing me again, but my eyes won't open. "Shh. I'll go easy," his breath wet on my ear. I can't move my body.

Jimmy Gallegos Snyder

Stations and Agency – Part One: This Time

Station: The place or position in which something or someone stands or is assigned to stand or remain.

Agency: The capacity of individuals to act independently and to make their own free choices.

•

I did not squint. Those rooms were barely dark-ish, even at their darkest. Never pitch black enough for this patient to get a proper sleep. Eyes always adjust. Fluorescent hallway light crept under the door. Medical equipment on the wall cast a tawny glow. The IV stand next to the bed, with its red digital readout, would flash when it was unhappy. Like faded neon, they all seemed just as tired as me. But, all together, they made it bright enough that I didn't need to squint in order to see.

Any apparatus that didn't engage the eyes, certainly ensnared the ears. Collectively a collaboration of mechanical music and air pressure played in a discordant loop.

Click-bling...squeak...

pssssst--psssssdtsshhr....

tick-tick-tick...BEEP-BEEP!

I was accustomed to those never-muted, hardly dark rooms by the time I was twelve. Up late, in that space, was commonplace. The call and response from both sides of the door was old hat. I was not an insomniac, per se. I may have allowed my ambient companions to keep me up late in order to sleep more during the day. As in during visiting hours. The company at night was just less complicated.

I was this asthmatic kid with seasonal allergies living in the smog capital of the USA. My medically compulsive mother had a collaborative relationship with our family doctor. They were the two primary ingredients in a recipe for repeat hospitalizations, like the rue and the chicken in a gumbo. Prior to this particular visit, that was my station. A sneeze and a cough become a wheeze and a deep cough, which lead to trips to the doctor's office for shots of adrenaline and breathing treatments. It ends at Brea Community Hospital. The BCH. That said, for all the same ol' same ol', this time was a wholly different experience. Serious. Real. And I didn't squint to see what was in the mirror staring back at me.

...Psssssssdtsshhr.

I was a frequent flyer. An extended stay customer. My well-practiced ears were always tuned into the corridor outside my room. This time there was a cardiac monitor in use a few rooms down, on the left. I could hear a ventilator in the room directly across the hall from mine.

...Psssssssdtsshhr.

Folks in those rooms were in very serious condition.

This time, so was I.

Pssssst...psssssssdtsshhr.

I had spent nearly equal time between that place and school, I knew, like clockwork, when the next nurse would be in to check my vitals. I knew the menu for each day of the week and that you could substitute any meal for grilled cheese or pb&j. I was on nickname basis with the janitorial staff, like Nathan Jenson. He had been a runner in high school. A runner, not a jogger. We called him "Jetman."

Claudia Cisneros was Sister "C" which sounded like the nickname for some super hip nun. I thought she was hip enough with her disco teased hair, thick eyeliner, Madonna gloves, and wider hoop earrings. But she wasn't a nun. She was one of eleven siblings. Third born. One-two-three, A-B-C, made her sister "C." You see? Jetman and Sister "C" called me "Jimmy Bean." They said I was skinny like a bean pole. There must have been some truth to that. Some of the kids at school called me "Jimmybones."

BEEP...BEEP, click-click

The TVs in some rooms had poor reception for channels nine and eleven. In the 80s that meant the Dodgers and the Lakers. Normally this would be a serious issue. No. Seriously. No Vin Scully or Chick Hearn, to me that meant no dice. It meant no IV, no vaporizer tent, no breathing treatments, no sub epidural injections. So, mom was no rookie when it came to making the arrangements. She handled admissions nurses the way a veteran tourist might lean on a hotel clerk for a better view of the courtyard and a couple extra tickets to the breakfast buffet. She could see to it that I had access to watch the sports which she had decided that I was too sick to play. This time I had been admitted via the emergency room. So, I got a room with poor reception. This time, I really didn't care.

•

Brakes screech. Impact number one, car strikes bike. Gravity shifts. Voice number one; "BRACE FOR IT!" More brakes. Voice number two; "Don't brace Jim...relax!" Impact number two, face strikes street.

•

Doctor Jack normally gets in at five, after his jog. I swear he used a frozen stethoscope and moved it like a glacier along my chest and then back.

"I was hoping that we could get you out of here today kiddo…deep breath…and again...but I'm still hearing that wheeze."

Dr. Jack was not a runner. He was an easy jogger. Sincerely, the license plate on his Datsun 260ZX spelled "E-Z-J-O-G-E-R." It seemed to me that a few of the attending nurses appreciated the ease of his jog. Some of the other employees did not. Sister "C" and Jetman were two who did not.

"What did that easy jogger have to say this morning Jimmy Bean? They didn't cut you free from this joint? You see that's why you can't trust a jogger. Especially an easy one. Legs were meant to run, man, not jog, certainly not lay in some damn hospital bed."

•

I give directions to my cousin Tom's house. One of the men standing around me breaks out of the huddle. I shut my eyes.

I open my eyes and my cousin Tom is squatting down next to me on the sidewalk. I can see his dad big Tom over his shoulder. Both stricken. I was always the whitest Mexican in the family. Not that day.

"Damn, Jimbo, what happened?"

"I dodged the first one…"

I give a little chuckle. Tom gives a nervous chuckle back. I shut my eyes.

I open my eyes. I'm in an ambulance.

"How you doin' there, Jim? Your cousin Tom told me your name is Jim. Is that right?"

I nod.

"How you doing, Jim? You hangin' in there?

"I feel sick."

I shut my eyes.

I open my eyes. I can hear my mom's voice.

"Why is he lying on a flat board?"

I see my stepdad.

"I'm so sorry." I say.

I throw up. I close my eyes.

•

Here's the rub: there really was this wheeze. A deep, resonant, wheeze which would linger in my lungs for weeks. It would drag on, at the end of an exhale, like a violin bow drawing a long-sustained note across a single string. It was always a minor note. Mom hated that note. To her it sounded like the emergency room. Like nights sitting on the bathroom floor with a hot shower steaming, child in her arms fighting to catch a proper breath. It possibly even conjured in her the quiet memory of her baby mouthing the word "mama" but only a gurgle sounding through the metal tube in his windpipe.

Of that metal tube and what to say about it? I cannot fathom the psychoneurotic imprint that such an experience leaves on a parent. How it might alter perceptions and responses. I can only speak to the imprint that an incision scar, like a third eye at the throat, leaves on an insecure child. Mine wasn't shaped like a lightning bolt or anything. But it received its own share of undesired attention. And it was a symbol of my vulnerability. My station.

Psssssssst...psssssssssdtsshhr

And of that wheeze and what to say about *it*? I've been debating its implications in my head for thirty-six years. I can say that it was a principal character; its own voice in the deliberations governing many of the circumstances of my life. It had a say in whether or not I played baseball, went to school, to the doctor, or the hospital. That said, and I'll say this again, this visit was different from those wheezy ones. This was more like that tube in the windpipe time. This visit I would take bits of it with me. And this time I would leave parts of myself behind.

This was serious. Like a heart attack or a collapsed lung. The degree of which was written in the face of every person who came in to visit. Doctor Jack stalled at the doorway, gray as an LA June morning. No jokes. No snickers. His eyes seeing me, perhaps honestly, for the first time. And my green eyes locked on his icy blues were definitely seeing him.

"Damn Jimmy Bean, they got you good, man"

Nathan Jetman wasn't afraid to look me in the face or tell me what was up.

"You make sure you keep that ice going, you hear me? You stay in that bed. I ain't gonna lie, man, you look like that cat Two Face from Batman. You read comics?"

Bling, bling.

Bling, bling.

Tick-tick-tick, BLEEP!

Nowhere to go. No cause to squint. At this point, I wasn't exactly sure how long I had been there. Three days? Four? Could it have been a week?

•

I was swimming at my cousin Tom's house. I made the quick three block bike ride from his house to mine, running the bike to a stop on the front lawn. I left a note on the kitchen table for my mom, hopped on the bike and sped back to beat the light at the intersection.

Yellow light.

I grasped the brakes. No answer. Gathering speed. I was barefoot. Do I try a Fred Flinstone? I tried. Wrong answer.

The light turned red.

I entered the intersection.

BEEP-BEEP-BEEP-BEEP

•

This time the BCH was different. Crazy. Or maybe it's just a crazy memory. My head was a TV set and someone else was having fun with the remote control. After I threw up in the trauma center at Queen of the Valley Hospital, I shut my eyes again. I opened them the next time and I was at the BCH. Had there been a second ambulance ride? I remember floating in and out of Hanna Barbarra-like dreams where caricatured faces were coming and going. Some of them I knew and some I didn't.

I know I rode a wheelchair to a CT scan. That was different. We had to go outside to get to the mobile trailer. The sun was an oven on my face. Then there was another wheelchair trip to the plastic surgeon.

"Nothing that we can say until that swelling goes down"

That was new.

ICE! There was lots of ice. Ice for my face. Ice chips only to eat. Was there ice dancing on TV?

Bleep....bling.

No need to squint. The night wasn't going anywhere. Neither was I. Besides, something told me that squinting would hurt. A lot. Like certain memories.

Tick...click

Cloth ice packs removed from the right side of my face had told a story of blood and tissue. They spoke of the parts of my face that the road could not claim but could no longer hold on to me. My pulse beat upon skin, pulled drum tight, above my right eye. I could feel in my skin the memory of flesh dissolving into asphalt. And I could hear the arguing internal voice just before moment of impact:

"BRACE FOR IT!"

"Don't brace! Relax."

There was no pain to speak of. The street felt softer than I expected. I had heeded the second voice and gone limp. And then numb.

Tick...bling...click...BEEP...BEEP...BEEP

It was dark-ish but I didn't need to squint to see that the right side of my face, from forehead to chin, nose to ear, a dividing line straight down the center, was a copper stained desert. There were three deep lacerations like dark black craters on an arid landscape. One crater between the lip and nose. Another at the eyebrow. The last one in the center of my cheek. A dime, a quarter, and a fifty-cent piece respectively.

Blood occupied the outside corner of my right eye, the area around which was distended and shades of yellow and purple. Bruises take several days to turn yellow. I had been there for several days. And then there was my right ear that I couldn't stop staring at. It was easily twice the size of the left; a giant red-capped mushroom.

I said to myself, "Damn Jimmy Bean. They got you good, man."

Then I laughed. Aloud. It hurt. A lot! The first real pain that I felt in the whole experience. It was good pain. It felt real. It felt like healing. It felt like freedom. Jetman was right. I did look like

Two Face from Batman. There in the mirror were two faces. And I didn't recognize either of them.

What I did recognize was that this time it was the real deal. Which meant that all the other times must have been bullshit. A station created by a collaborative doctor and a medically compulsive mother.

There had been two voices in my head.

"Brace for it."

"No, Relax."

The second was mine. The first was hers. Agency versus the station. Agency may have saved my life that day. After ten days they sent me home. And I never took a bed in that place again.

ShuJen Walker

Be Brave

From the doorway of my childhood home, I watch him play. At 3 years old, big brown eyes, and curly hair, my heart melts. Dressed in a Hulk T-Shirt, navy blue slacks, and Paw Patrol sneakers, he rolls around on the artificial lawn pretending it a jungle gym.

With five minutes left, I shout, "Bud, are you ready for a fun day?"

"Vroom…vroom." He focuses on the wheels of the toy trains, ignoring me like he always does.

Four minutes left. "Am I forgetting something?" I dig inside his blue bear-shaped backpack and fiddle around. Diapers, wipes, sippy cup, change of clothes in case he has a blowout, and Doritos, his favorite snack – all here.

I double-check the contents of my briefcase, grab my purse, and approach him. "Bud, are you ready to go bye-bye?"

He scoops up his trains, stands, and takes my hand.

"You're going to have a fun day," I exclaim as we walk to the end of the driveway in time to see the small bus inching its way down our street. The roaring engine makes my heart beat faster.

"See the bus?" I point. "Can you say, *bus*? Yellooow…busss…" I repeat until my cheeks feel the heat.

He kicks a pebble. "Babaa…dadaaa."

The bus pulls up, and the driver steps off. "Ma'am, is this little Trevor?" He grins from ear to ear.

I nod, tears welling in my eyes, throat dry.

"Nothing to worry about, ma'am. I'll get him to school safely." The driver takes his hand, and they disappear inside.

Strapped snugly in the first row, my boy's beaming smile brightens my day. The engine rumbles and I wave, blowing kisses goodbye. He waves back. My heart leaps. Joyful tears form. Is he communicating? I wave harder, voice cracking as I shout goodbye, goodbye – that is until a butterfly flies away from the window and he stops swatting at it, then goes back to playing trains.

I sulk, then laugh at the absurdity, my stomach knotting as the bus takes off. "What am I doing? I can't." I rush to my vehicle and freeze. The silhouette of his empty car seat burns a hole through the tinted window, and into my heart. I close my eyes. "The first day of school for autistic children, be brave."

Fiancé Visa

"Would you like the Chinese or American breakfast?"

I stare at the flight attendant with a confused look. "My English, no good."

The blond woman smiles then unwraps the foil covering the trays of food, revealing eggs and bacon in one hand, and porridge and fish in the other. My eyes point to the combo I know best. Stomach growling, I dig in, making sure not to choke on the small bones.

"Good morning folks, 30 minutes to our final destination. We'll arrive at approximately 7:45 a.m. Pacific Standard Time."

As the translated version of the message plays, my heart thumps. My dream of finally seeing Howard after two years is about to come true. I could still feel the softness of his lips the last time we kissed. I close my eyes, lost in that day.

"I've got orders to be stationed back in the states."

Howard broke the news to me one evening, while we ate dan gao and drank cha during our visit to Rongxing Garden Park.

"What about me?" I turned away from him, hands covering my eyes.

"Fiancé Visa. I will apply when I get back home. It should only take a few months." He adjusted the collar of his Air Force uniform and smiled.

I shrunk back in terror. "But your wife? You two will make it work?"

"No." He shook his head and gently touched my hand. "I told you before. We've been separated for months."

"Your son?"

His eyebrows furrowed. "We talked about him living with us. Did you change your mind?"

"Of course not. I'm just afraid he won't like me. Your family won't like me. I'm not American. They may not understand…"

"Don't worry." Howard wrapped his arms around my entire body, embracing me in his warmth, and kissing my forehead. "Everything will be fine."

A week later, he left. My heart broke.

"Tea, Miss?"

The flight attendant appears out of nowhere, and I stare with blank eyes, until she places a cup of hot tea on my tray. The steam hits my nose and I take a sip. The bitter taste of the freshly brewed green liquid transports me thousands of miles back home to Taipei.

"Why you want to leave, Ajenna? Go so far away from family?" My sister asked while stacking loaves of bread on the shelf.

"Dad, stepmom, they don't care about me." I passed her another loaf.

"They do care."

"Then why did they move to a different house and not tell me? That was the third time. I had to ask neighbors where they were. You know how embarrassing that was?"

"They're old. They don't think about those things."

"Why have they never met Howard?"

"They don't like foreigners too much."

"They could have at least saw me off." I squished one of the loaves out of frustration.

My sister glanced away.

"It's because they don't understand why I divorced Aco. They don't care that he abused me. Now I found a man who cares about me, and they don't like it because he's American. He treats me better than anyone here. That's why I'm leaving."

"Ajenna, please…forgive them." She squeezed my hand. "Don't forget us."

"Passengers, we have made our final descent into San Diego. Please take your seats. Flight Attendants, prepare for landing."

I close my eyes and pray to Guanyin to watch over me in my new stage of life.

The plane lands, and my stomach drops. New home. New life. I drag my feet as they usher everyone off the plane and into U.S. Customs. Spoken English fills my ears and walls of people who don't look like me, swallow my body. I'm terrified and want to turn back, but where to go? Everywhere I turn a slurry of foreign letters blinds my vision. I feel lost inside.

"Passport?"

I stare at the border agent and hold up my papers.

"Fiancé Visa?" He scans the document, then stamps it. "Welcome to the U.S."

I follow the crowd out through the double doors and into a long brightly lit hallway. The doors slam shut, and I jump. No turning back. I must move forward.

“It’s going to be ok.” I repeat to myself. My heart beats faster as I turn the corner. Amongst the sea of blue uniforms, I see him. Tears fill my eyes and I run.

James Patrick Rodey Editors' Choice Award - Prose

Jesla

Every time it thumped, Jesla's stomach coiled. A vibration she hadn't felt in forever, resonated through the walls, reminding her she was one step closer to going home. *I'm coming!* She echoed.

"So, everyone, in the year 2525, this is how Gregg Industry plays a vital role in establishing, creating, and sustaining this technologically advanced metropolis we live in." The tour guide clapped. "*Museum of the Exotic* is where our tour ends. Follow me to your busses."

As they headed to the security checkpoint, Jesla squirmed knowing this would be her only chance to take back what they stole. She followed her class out the door, then made an immediate right down the intersecting hallway.

"Where are you going?" Yelled the teacher.

She walked faster, then purposely bumping into a worker carrying a load of papers.

"Sorry," the worker smiled. "Clumsy me."

Jesla waved and continued walking as her body took on the characteristics of the worker, becoming her doppelganger. Admiring her new disguise, she ran her fingers through her long, wavy brown hair and adjusted her coke bottle glasses. The light blue color lab coat matched her eyes; however, the smell of tuna breath made her puke in her mouth.

"Have you seen a girl about…?" Her teacher's voice carried down the hall.

Not wanting to hear the response, Jesla turned down another hallway and then took several more turns until she came up to Room 6, labeled, "Objects of Unknown Origin."

I'm here, my love. She accessed the room with her badge and entered. Instantly, her eyes lit up at the sight of her golden green box lying on a table behind a thick glass wall. The rest of her belongings laid scattered on display, however, all she cared about was her precious beacon, the only way home.

She placed her hands flat on the glass wall and allowed the sticky sensors at the edge of her fingertips to intertwine with the structure, exploring its chemical makeup. Immediately locking onto its vibration, her body became one with its frequency and she effortlessly slid through to the other side. Grabbing the box and holding him close, she muttered. *It's time to go home.*

Again, she locked onto the vibrations of the glass to leave, but half-way through, a high-pitched whining pierced her ears. The alarm disrupted her energy flow, causing the glass to trap her in between its structure, head on one side, body on the other. She squirmed and pounded the glass as a gaseous gray substance rose from the floor vents snuffing out the air.

The door swung open, two guards in blue uniforms entered the room. They hit the red button on the wall and the glass faded out.

Jesla collapsed, coughing nonstop. They rushed to her side. "Hold on, Ms. Lang. Help is on the way."

No! I can't get caught. Hysterical at the thought, she accidentally cycled through several past transformations until changing back into the scantily dressed college girl. The guard's eyes opened wide and they both snatched their hands away from her exposed skin.

"Imposter!" They drew their weapons. "Don't move."

She slowly stood, hands up. Swaying like a drunk, she stepped forward and opened her mouth wide. Green slime ejected from her tongue, hitting the guards in the face. Sizzling sounds erupted as the acid ate through their skin.

She ran past them, out the door and into the hallway where dozens of uniformed guards surrounded her.

"It's ok, Jesla. My name is Dr. Frank. We've been waiting for you." A voice came through a loudspeaker. "We have much to talk about. I want to first welcome you to our planet."

Glaring light from a nearby window caught her attention and she wobbled taking a half step.

"Nerve gas, for your species. It incapacitates you."

She ignored him and rushed towards the window.

"Stop her!" Dr. Frank yelled.

Too late, she dove out the window and somersaulted five stories down landing on her feet. She then ran through the woods to the Teleport Transit Center, Station 9, and purposely bumped into an old lady, instantly assuming her identity. Locating the shortest line to a teleportation device, she ran up to the front, coughing and pointing to her heart. It took a moment for the dense hunk to get it.

"Sure, you can go before me, ma'am." He backed up.

"Attention everyone." A hologram appeared in the sky. "This is Dr. Frank. As you know in this beautiful metropolis of ours, it is not always without problems. Today, we have a fugitive wanted for questioning." Her school photo flashed across the sky. "She is armed and dangerous. Whoever turns her in, will be highly rewarded. We will bring your entire family into Test City. Think about what that could mean for your future generations."

Panicking, Jesla immediately shifted back into the college girl look, and jumped into the portal.

Music blasted. "Welcome to the twenty-fifth century way to travel." A jolly commercial spiel and wacky dancers displayed across the screen. "Punch in your location please."

Jesla typed in the ten-digit teleportation code and waited. The timer spun, but nothing happened.

"We apologize, the system is experiencing technical difficulties, please be patient." The computer spoke.

Raucous outside grabbed her attention as guards yelled for her to come out.

Jesla banged on the keypad until the numbers went through, and every cell in her body ripped apart, then came together as a whole. As she stepped out, a blow to the head knocked her unconscious.

When she woke, she found herself trapped in a concrete room with no doors. Her box was gone. Suddenly, the walls dissolved, and she found herself facing an audience of lab coats, with no visible barrier separating them.

"Ladies and Gentlemen, meet the owner of the belongings in Room 6, origin and species unknown, possibly from a planet in the Alpha Aphotic Galaxy. Entered our Solar System about four years ago. Escaped and assumed the identity of a college student. She is skilled at cloning. We are dealing with a highly intelligent species."

Jesla's eyes opened wide as the man picked up her box. She perked her ears, listening for the thumping, but heard nothing. *Is he dead?* She put her hands up to her head, pacing.

"Jesla, what's inside? What's so important, you'd risk your life to steal it?"

Steal it, it's mine! She pumped her fist.

A hand shot up in the audience. "Why isn't she talking?"

One of the lab coats entered the barrier and placed a pen and paper on the table. Jesla studied his interaction with the barrier, sensing its natural frequency. She vibrated accordingly and tried to follow him out, but not perfectly synched, she hit the wall. The green light shimmered, instantly communicating with her skin. ***Friend***, she heard a voice and immediately backed away, processing the information.

"Write what you want."

I WANT TO GO HOME! She held up the pad.

"Where is home?" Dr. Frank shook the box.

DON'T SHAKE HIM!

"Him who?"

When Dr. Frank wouldn't stop, rage and anger blinded her. She put her hands up to the invisible wall and concentrated, locking onto its frequency. The green light, a life force of its own, ***Friend***, flickered and guided her until she slid through to the other side.

Everyone gasped and backed away. She snatched the box out of Dr. Frank's ran into the crowd of screaming lab coats, instantly taking the shape of a man. Sirens sounded.

Jesla found a teleporter in one of the rooms and jumped in.

"Welcome to the traveling century state of the art…"

She pounded the keypad in frustration. It finally worked and the doors swung open to her college dorm. She hurried to her room and grabbed her toy robot, then ran to another teleporter. She dialed the number to get outside Test City.

The computer beeped. "The number you dialed does not exist in Test City. Check your number and try again."

Worthless contraption!

Suddenly the teleportation station disappeared, men in blue surrounded her, weapons drawn.

"It's over Jesla, you're not going anywhere." Dr. Frank put his hands together. "I own the grid. I own the machines. I own this world!"

She held out her toy robot, its brown hair wild, feet dangling.

"Cute, but what are you going to do with that?"

Taking a chance! She opened the box, pulled out the thumping robotic heart, and gently placed it into the chest of the toy bot. Instantly, the bot grew to over ten feet tall, picked her up and shot up in the air like a rocket. She looked down at the Earthlings, happy to be going home.

A loud boom erupted, lights flashed, and then everything went dark.

The Sweet Voice

The door swings open, and I run outside. My firm shoes thump the pavement, as the cool breeze whistles in my ears. I giggle in freedom, then drop to my knees rustling around on the soft blades of grass, creating cackling sparks of static electricity. *Vroom...vroom!* I enjoy the sounds of my toy cars ramming together.

"Bud, are you ready for a fun day?"

Her sweet voice muffles against the whizzing sounds of the spinning wheels on my toy car. The blending of colors put me in a trancelike state, creating an optical illusion, giving me a false sense of speed. I thirst for more and spin them faster and faster until the tones in her expression fade to background noise.

"Bud, are you ready to go bye-bye?" Her pitch sharpens, awakening my inner core as I recognize the word, 'bye-bye.'

Bye-Bye! Bye-Bye! I repeat in my mind. *I'm going on a car ride.* I stand and take her hand. The gentle touch of her skin put me at ease, and I squeeze back.

"You're going to have a fun day! See the bus? Can you say, yellow bus?"

"Babaa…dadaaa," I respond.

Squeaking and hissing sounds grow louder as huge wheels larger than me stop in front. A man steps off.

"Ma'am, is this little Trevor?"

"Yes," she mutters.

"Nothing to worry about ma'am. I'll get him to school safely."

The driver takes my hand, helps me up the stairs, and sits me next to the window. I look out to see her waving. I wave back, until flapping sounds catch my attention. A butterfly appears, and I swat for it to move. When it finally disappears, I look around, but no longer see her.

EXTRAS

Glossary

Free Verse: a poetic form not dictated by structure or rhyme scheme; it often follows a more natural speech pattern, using line breaks to control the flow.

Ghazal: five to fifteen couplets, each of the lines being the same length. Both lines in the first couplet and second line of subsequent couplets end in the same word. The final couplet traditionally refers to the author, often including the author's own name.

Haiku: A traditional Japanese haiku is a three-line poem written in a 5/7/5 syllable count. They often focus on themes of nature.

Sestina: a complex, thirty-nine-line poem featuring the intricate repetition of end-words in six stanzas and an envoi.

Sonnet: traditionally a fourteen-line poem in iambic pentameter. Although the Shakespearean Sonnet is arguably the most known, the Petrarchan Sonnet is the most common.

Tanka: a thirty-one-syllable poem, traditionally written in a single unbroken line, but is better known in its five-line, 5/7/5/7/7 syllable count form.

Contributors' Notes

Elizabeth Aguilar is an English major at Grossmont College and spoke at New Voices in Spring 2019.

Calleigh Backrak is originally from Sacramento, California, but after her enlisted in the U.S. Navy, she decided to make San Diego her home. She lives a very happy and satisfying existence with her boyfriend, Ignas, and her dog, a goofy little pug named Dutch. She currently is a student at Grossmont College, and plans to go to San Diego State in the fall of 2021.

Tasha Bonsignore is a native San Diegan and artist.

Shahin Elihu is a student at Grossmont College taking English classes. He reads Persian poetry.

Beth Ferris is a continuing student in the Grossmont College Creative Writing Program.

Chelsey Gable is an English major at Grossmont College and is working towards earning a certificate in Creative Writing. She writes creative non-fiction and poetry in regard to a variety of topics that range from her experience as a single mother, to feminism, and others of life's oddities.

Angelica Garcia Diaz is a first-generation student at Grossmont College who is currently double majoring in Physics and English. Although she thoroughly enjoys the horror and thriller genre above all else, her works tend to revolve around romance, everyday life, and activism.

F.C. George has been a writer for many years without knowing it. Just very recently, a few years ago, in a creative writing class at Grossmont College, that talent was brought to light again. George is a local and resides in East County and works as an artist.

Reina Hearts is a shy San Diego native coming to terms with being the female version of her deceased father. While her FPLOON persona only writes in haikus compared to her non-haiku style of poetry, both personas express a sense of unconventional surrealism and randomness within their semi-personal self-reflections. When writing and/or being an interim editor for the Acorn Review isn't on the agenda, she'd be either playing video games, binge-watching animation, or styling her long nails.

Tay Heylman - I took this photo on February 16th, 2020. It was just before sunset and I loved the way the sun hit the ocean around that time. Before, I took it, it was bright and I could see all the colors of everything in front and around me, then once I took it, it became a beautiful black and golden picture.

Merrienne Jimenez says after several fickle years, she began exploring writing at Grossmont College. She will continue to do so at University of California, San Diego.

Rebecca Kanter wrote and illustrated a book made of construction paper and tape about a family's summertime visit to "The Fer" when she was in second grade. Now she writes historical fiction and stories about motherhood. She wishes that she could meet her ancestors.

Fabian Diaz Luevano says in his artistic work, he mainly studies natural objects using primarily graphite and charcoal and occasionally photography. He is also a student of Arabic at Grossmont College and works on honing technical skills in an illustration course at Cuyamaca College.

Michele Magnuson (see editor's note)

Ricardo S. Martinez has a BA from SDSU. He was apprenticed from Glover Davis, Gary Soto, Carolyn Force, Alurista (all for poetry) and Eizabeth Chater (fiction), graduating in 1977. He has also been a published contributor to four numismatic books concerning error coins and numismatic varieties. He is a native San Diegan. In 1988, he was privileged to be selected by KPBS radio to read some of my poems on the air.

Cameron McGowan is an artist/author focusing on mental health awareness through their work.

Damia Meglasson - There are those who fear death and those who fear life. Fearing both can be a negative force in one's life, or they can harness that fear and choose to use it as a creative basis, a sort of philosophy to base their stories around be it subtle or discernible.

Mick Miles grew up in Hawai'i, where he was exposed to a tradition of storytelling so ingrained in the culture that the term "talking story" is synonymous with conversation. Mick now lives in San Diego with his girlfriend and two kids, yet he never leaves Maui in his fiction.

Tim Mountain is an East County of San Diego Photographer and Grossmont College Alum. He works for the San Diego Public Library.

Jay M. Mower, a retired marketing executive, advertising professor and management consultant, lives in San Diego and has written over 40 published poems, three chapbooks and has a full-length poetry book scheduled 2020.

Duncan Mullis is 20 years old. His hobbies include hiding in the dark of his room and hissing whenever someone draws open the curtains. He lives in his head, but his head can normally be found in El Cajon, California.

Jessica Nelson lives in Ramona, Ca, her hometown. She has two rescues, a dog named Pecas and a cat name Kristy-Ann. She also has a little leopard gecko named bean. Jessica is pursuing a career in the culinary art, while working as a cook and attending Grossmont College. She has always enjoyed cooking and aspires to one day be a chef. Jessica's hobbies include writing, playing tennis, and gardening. She has a slight obsession with house plants and wants to turn her room into her own personal jungle.

E. R. O'Connor was recently featured at the Grossmont Literary Arts Festival Student Reading of 2019 for her poetry. She draws her inspiration

Dee Richards was born and raised in San Diego, is a parent, an intersectional feminist, a proud member of the LGBTQ+

community, a student, and sometimes self-identifies as a writer and editor.

Hannah Ross is an English major at Grossmont College while having her own photography business. Her photography is inspired by old black and white film photographers such as Diane Arbus, Les Krims, Garry Winogrand, and Bill Owens.

Jimmy Gallegos Snyder is currently living in La Mesa California during the strangest time of his life. He lives in an apartment in the Village with his wife and their two daughters. He owns a small bread distribution route and enjoys writing poetry and narrative non- fiction.

Edward Michael Supranowicz has had artwork and poems published in journals in the US and other countries. Both sides of his family worked in the coalmines and steel mills of Appalachia.

Talahni Turin's poem "I Praise" narrates the significant history and unique hair styles of Black women's hair.

Bella Van Tassel is an 18-year-old who was born and raised in San Diego. She began art at the age of 14 and started art shows at the age of 16. She started selling her art at the age of 17 and has her art in over 100 homes in over 25 states.

Dan Vidri is an amateur photographer. He lives in El Cajon and is currently attending Grossmont College while working full time in the insurance industry.

ShuJen Walker is a Grossmont College student who completed her first YA Fantasy Novel. She also writes flash fiction and short stories in many genres. An Electrical Engineer by trade, ShuJen is a busy mama of two, who's passion is art and writing

Ingrid Yoxsimer is a current Grossmont student working on her English degree in order to one day teach the subject at a high school level. She is heavily inspired by writers such as William Carlos Williams, Oscar Wilde, Jim Morrison, and Bob Dylan. She recently read her piece "Love Poem" at Grossmont's 2019 New Voices Literary Event.

www.ingramcontent.com/pod-product-compliance
Lightning Source LLC
Chambersburg PA
CBHW070956180726
48291CB00004B/1325

* 9 7 8 1 9 4 3 8 9 9 1 2 8 *